LOCOMOTIVE PAPERS   LP 253

THE WESTBURY
TO
SALISBURY LINE

Colin G. Maggs

On Upton Scudamore Bank a 56XX class 0-6-2T No. 5689 assists at the rear of the train headed by No. 7023 *Penrice Castle*, the 1.00 pm Cardiff–Brighton comprised of SR coaching stock, 2nd July, 1955.
R. E. Toop

THE OAKWOOD PRESS

© Colin G. Maggs, 2024

ISBN 978-0-85361-774-7

First Published in the United Kingdom, 2024.

Printed by
Claro Print, Office 26, 27, 1 Spiersbridge Way
Thornliebank, Glasgow G46 8NG

Acknowledgements

Thanks are due to the staff of the Bath Record Office, the Institution of Civil Engineers, Peter Blackmore, Pete Foreman, John Mann and Howard Wilkie, with special thanks to Colin Roberts.

Wylye station. after closure in 1955, looking sad on 27th April, 1963. The main building remains minus the chimney, as do the water tank on the left and the water meter just left of the building. *Author*

Front cover upper: At Salisbury, rebuilt West Country class Pacific No. 34101 *Hartland* about to be uncoupled and replaced by a WR engine to take it on to South Wales, 11th October, 1962. On the right is unrebuilt No. 34106 *Lydford* having worked a stopper from Waterloo.
Revd. Alan Newman

Lower On Upper Scudamore Bank 4-6-0 No. 6997 *Bryn-Ivor Hal*l with a Cardiff to Portsmouth train banked by 0-6-2T No. 5689, 9th July, 1955. The tethered goat seems to be a locomotive enthusiast. *R. E. Toop*

Published by
The Oakwood Press, 54-58 Mill Square, Catrine, KA5 6RD
01290 551122   www.stenlake.co.uk

Contents

Introduction 5

Chapters

One	First Proposals	7
Two	The Bristol, South Wales & Southampton Union Railway	31
Three	Salisbury Market House Railway	33
Four	Description of the Line	35
Five	Locomotives	83
Six	Timetables & Train Working	105
Seven	Signalling & Permanent Way	123
Eight	Accidents	131
Nine	First World War Military Branches	139

Bibliography 147

Appendices

One	Westbury Shed Allocation	148
Two	Salisbury Shed Allocation	150
Three	Westbury Ironworks Locomotives	150
Four	Authorised Hours of Bank Engines 1954	151
Five	Hand-Book of Railway Stations	151
Six	Logs of Runs	152
Seven	Traffic Dealt With at Stations	154

Index 158

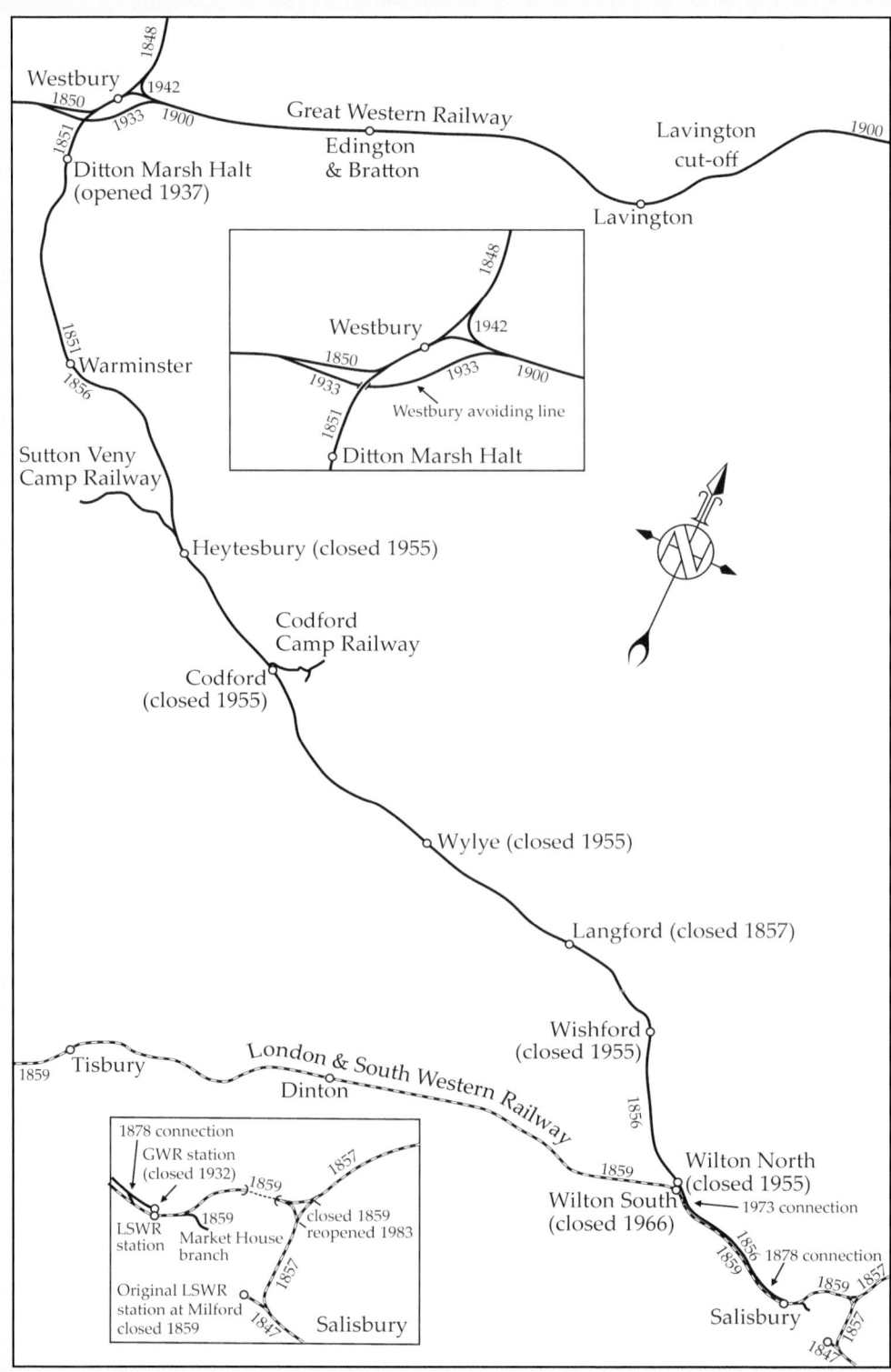

Introduction

Initially Salisbury was unlucky in the provision of railways. Although only 82¼ miles from London by road, it was first served by an extension of the London & Southampton Railway making a distance, from their London terminus at Nine Elms via Eastleigh, of 95.6 miles.

Although the Act of Parliament was passed on 4th July, 1844 building the line proved far from straightforward: landowners proved obstructive and property prices had to go to arbitration. Then, instead of employing the reliable Thomas Brassey, the contract of the delightfully named Hoof & Hill was accepted, it being £18,000 below that of its competitors. Because flooding had made Salisbury desperately short of food, the incomplete 24 mile long line to Milford on the outskirts of Salisbury saw the first train from Nine Elms leave at 7.00 am on 21st January, 1847 and arrive Salisbury at 11.15 am with railway officials and 'all the London papers'. The election on Monday 25th January, 1847 deferred the opening for coal traffic for two days. Salisbury is not near a coalfield, and coal was an important commodity and expensive to transport, so there was presumably considerable relief, when on 27th January, 1847 ninety tons of coal arrived for distressed households. The next day saw three trains arrive carrying beef, mutton, pork, flour, butter, cheese and animal fodder. The branch opened to passenger traffic on 1st March, 1847, a celebratory public dinner being held at the White Hart, Salisbury that evening.

The London & South Western Railway, (as the London & Southampton had become on 4th June, 1839), having reached Salisbury, the broad gauge Great Western Railway (GWR) was concerned that this standard gauge LSWR would trespass into what it considered its territory. To prevent this incursion, at a meeting in Warminster on 9th July, 1844, the Wilts & Somerset Railway was proposed. This was a line planned by Brunel to run from the Great Western Railway at Thingley Junction near Chippenham, to Salisbury, with branches to Bradford-on-Avon, Frome and Devizes. As the LSWR was advancing westwards along the south coast, in an effort to block this move, the plan was modified to include Weymouth. The Bill incorporating the Wilts Somerset & Weymouth Railway (WSWR) was passed on 30th June, 1845.

As this was the year of the Railway Mania when so many railway schemes were proposed, there was a severe shortage of cash for investment, thus construction could not start immediately, though the line had been marked out by October 1845. Although the line was a protegé of the GWR, it was thought that a local company would attract subscriptions more readily. This theory proved unfounded, so on 14th March, 1850 the GWR took over the WSWR giving its shareholders 4 per cent guaranteed stock in lieu of their ordinary shares. This move was confirmed by Parliament on 3nd July, 1851, and on 31st July, 1854 a further Act was obtained to allow more time to complete the line.

The GWR's line to Salisbury opened to coal traffic on 11th June, 1856 and passenger traffic began on 30th June, 1856. As the GWR approached the city from the west, the distance from London via Swindon and Chippenham was 136.3 miles, this fact helping to prove that 'GWR' stood for 'Great Way Round'. When the London & South Western Railway opened its direct line from Andover to Salisbury on 1st May, 1857 the LSWR's mileage was reduced to 83.8, while the GWR's Lavington cut-off brought that company's mileage down to 121.1.

Unusual features of the GWR's Salisbury branch were that it began life as a single-track, broad gauge, dead-end branch, later to become a double-track standard gauge through main line, while in September 1955 it became one of the first main lines in the country to lose most of its intermediate stations. Other rarities included a station raised on jacks and another with one of the shortest platforms in the kingdom.

The GWR Salisbury Ambulance Class circa 1914. *Author's collection*

Chapter One

First Proposals

A railway between Westbury and Salisbury was first mentioned in the 1820s when William James projected and surveyed a horse-worked line from Bristol to Salisbury and Southampton, but the scheme proved abortive. The London & Southampton Railway opened throughout in 1839 and the GWR completed its route from London to Bristol in 1841. Thus a considerable tract of country between the two ports of Southampton and Bristol were left devoid of rail communication, the area having important market towns such as Melksham, Devizes, Radstock, Frome, Warminster, Salisbury, Yeovil, Dorchester and Weymouth.

In 1844 as the Railway Mania was gaining momentum, in order to counter the LSWR's extension line, authorised by the LSWR Act of 4th July, 1844, from Bishopstoke (Eastleigh) to Salisbury, the GWR proposed a line from Thingley, two miles west of Chippenham, to Salisbury. On 31st May, 1844 a meeting in the council chamber, Salisbury saw the proposal of the Great Western Junction Railway, a broad gauge line from the GWR at Thingley, just west of Chippenham serving Bradford, Devizes, Frome and Salisbury. With a length of 52 miles, Brunel believed it could be built economically at £10,000 a mile as there was no need for tunnels, deep cuttings or heavy embankments. Except for the Frome branch which ventured into Somerset, the line would be entirely within Wiltshire. The GWR was willing to guarantee a minimum interest of three and a half per cent and was prepared to purchase up to half of the shares if they were not taken up. It was anticipated that the line would be either double track, or single if worked on the atmospheric principle. The scheme was authorised by the Wilts, Somerset & Weymouth Railway Act of 30th June, 1845, while the competitive LSWR Salisbury & Yeovil Extension Act of 22nd July, 1848 sanctioned a direct line to Salisbury from Basingstoke via Andover. Two other companies were planning to open up the territory: the LSWR sought to build a line from Basingstoke via Newbury to Swindon and the Bristol & Exeter Railway desired to make a line from Durston to Weymouth.

In December 1844 the recently-established Railway Department of the Board of Trade gave its decision entirely in favour of the GWR scheme, whereupon the two companies signed an agreement on 16th January, 1845 pledging themselves to end hostilities. The Wilts & Somerset Railway, (W&S) nominally an independent company, was to build a line from Thingley to Salisbury and branches to Devizes, Bradford and

Frome with a 'coal branch' to Radstock. At Salisbury the Wilts & Somerset was to connect with the LSWR's branch from Bishopstoke (Eastleigh), so that, as the directors worded it in their report of August 1844, 'communication between Bristol, Bath, Southampton, Portsmouth and the Isle of Wight would be superior in every respect to any railway which could be made between Basingstoke and Swindon'. At a time of cut-throat competition between the various railway companies, the W&S had been set up in an attempt to block the LSWR's move westwards into territory which the GWR believed was its own.

The first meeting of the Wilts & Somerset Railway was held at the Bath Arms Inn, Warminster on 9th July, 1844, Walter Long MP being in the chair. I. K. Brunel had submitted plans to the meeting and judged £650,000 sufficient to cover every expense. It was resolved that a provisional committee be formed with Walter Long as chairman, the capital of £650,000 to be divided into 13,000 shares of £50 each and a deposit of £2.10*s*. 0*d*. required on each share. (Initially shares were not bought outright, but various 'calls' made to pay for construction as it progressed).

Charles Alexander Saunders, the GWR secretary, submitted to the meeting two plans by which the subscription of the required capital could probably be obtained on the security of his company as guarantors of a fixed percentage, W&S subscribers being pledged from GWR funds 3½ per cent on capital and after paying this amount, any surplus would be equally divided between W&S shareholders and the GWR. An alternative idea was that investors received on each £50 share, half the dividend payable on a GWR £50 share, under guarantee that it would never be less than 3½ per cent per annum on capital. In either case, Saunders said that the GWR would be lessees of the line in consideration of payments to be made to shareholders as above; furthermore, the GWR was prepared to subscribe up to half the capital.

The W&S resolved that it was expedient to accept the second scheme and in return for this support, the GWR was to have a perpetual lease and rights to work the line. A month later, Saunders informed the W&S that his directors had decided to offer a guarantee of 4 per cent, hoping to assist the project by inducing local inhabitants to subscribe.

On 23nd October, 1844 the provisional committee meeting at the George Inn, Frome, suggested that in addition to the branches to Devizes, Bradford, Frome and Radstock, there be a branch to Yeovil and Weymouth, this obviating the need of a Bristol & Exeter branch to that watering place. Brunel estimated the necessary capital needed to be £1½m. In view of the amended aims of the W&S, the meeting altered the name to the more applicable Wilts, Somerset & Weymouth Railway (WSWR). The use of the atmospheric principle was quietly forgotten.

On 19th November, 1844 the GWR directors subscribed on their company's behalf for the 10,000 shares not taken in order to raise the number of shares to 22,500, that is three-quarters of the capital required by Parliament. The *London Gazette* of 31st December, 1844 reported that the Board of Trade was in favour of the WSWR subject to the condition of applying to Parliament in a future session for a line from Bradford towards Bath. On 28th April, 1845 the WSWR made a leasing agreement with the GWR for a minimum dividend guarantee from its funds of 4 per cent with an increase of a half per cent on the proportion to any dividend exceeding 8 per cent per annum on the amount of its own capital. When the Parliamentary Railway Committee considered the WSWR Bill the estimated cost per mile was £12,000.

The Wilts, Somerset & Weymouth Railway Act, 8-9 Vic. Cap. 53 was passed on 30th June, 1845 authorising a line to be built from the GWR at Thingley to Salisbury, with branches to Weymouth, Devizes, Bradford, Radstock, Sherborne and Bridport, the gauge to be that of the GWR, and powers were given to lease the line to that company. Authorised capital was £1½m with borrowing powers of £½m, the GWR being permitted to subscribe and guarantee interest up to 5 per cent. The WSWR was to have twelve directors of whom initially four were to be appointed by the GWR. The Act stipulated that the WSWR was to apply to Parliament during the forthcoming Session to make a line from Trowbridge towards Bath.

The first meeting of the WSWR directors after the passing of the Act was held at Trowbridge on 1st August, 1845, Walter Long being appointed chairman and Sir John Wither Awdry, deputy chairman. Brunel was selected to be the company's engineer with R. J. Ward as resident engineer for the section Thingley–Salisbury–Frome–Radstock. A corporate seal was ordered – the quartered arms of Devizes, Salisbury, Wells and Weymouth.

Little time was wasted and by October 1845 the line was staked out to Salisbury. Brunel had arranged three contracts: Thingley–Staverton; Staverton–Heytesbury and Heytesbury–Salisbury. The directors required the parties tendering to accept that they would co-operate in preventing Sunday labour in every instance where it was not an indispensable necessity. The WSWR was certainly interested in the religious welfare of its employees and offered the Bishop of Salisbury £150 towards a subscription for appointing one or more chaplains to attend to the 'spiritual conditions' of the navvies.

Further evidence that the directors looked after the welfare of their men was found in the condition that the contractors were required to bind themselves not to pay navvies at beer shops or public houses. The 'truck or tommy system' whereby payment was made either in goods, or tickets which could be exchanged for goods, was banned as it led to the exploitation of the men. Supplies offered at truck shops were often bad, highly priced and of short weight. At Quidhampton, two miles west of Salisbury, navvies were given tickets to the value of what they supposed was about half their wages, but when they came to be paid some received less than a shilling in cash for a week's work. In April 1846 they struck as it was a time of extensive railway building, labour was scarce and they could have easily secured a new job on the Basingstoke to Salisbury line.

The *Salisbury & Winchester Journal* of 24th April, 1847 reported:

> It would be much better to give 1s. 6d. only a day in hard cash, to be disposed of at the pleasure of a labourer, than, at present, to give him 2s. 6d. to 3s. a day and then send the poor fellow to a Tommy Shop for all that he required, thus leaving him at the end of a week's hard work with little or nothing to receive.

A slightly different aspect of the humanitarian side of the WSWR directors was that on 19th May, 1846 they approved the establishment of a sick club for men engaged on the works.

At the half-yearly meeting in August 1848 it was reported that considerable amount of work had been executed on the line between Westbury and Salisbury but work near Salisbury had been suspended until that near Westbury was more advanced.

Captain Meredith, chief constable of Wiltshire, recommended an increase of six men to his force as a direct result of the influx of railway navvies. A riot took place at Westbury on 14th July, 1849, some of the police being seriously assaulted. The contractors Messrs Roach &

> **Wilts, Somerset, and Weymouth Railway.**
>
> NOTICE IS HEREBY GIVEN,—That the HALF-YEARLY ORDINARY MEETING of the SHAREHOLDERS in this Company will be held on TUESDAY, the 29th day of February inst., at Two o'Clock, p.m., precisely, at the WHITE LION HOTEL, in the City of Bath.
>
> And NOTICE IS HEREBY FURTHER GIVEN,—That the BOOKS kept by the Company for the Registration of Transfer of Shares will be CLOSED on and from TUESDAY, the 15th day of February inst., to and including TUESDAY, the 29th day of February, inst.
>
> WALTER LONG, Chairman.
> W. O'BRIEN, Secretary.
> Trowbridge, 1st February, 1848.

Announcement of half-yearly meeting. *Wiltshire Independent* 24th February, 1848

Pilditch promised, in conjunction with R. J. Ward the resident engineer, to discharge the men at fault and alter the arrangement so that the sub-contractor Taylor, paid his men earlier on a Saturday.

Meanwhile in 1846 a Supplementary Act was obtained moving the junction of the Weymouth and Salisbury lines from Upton Scudamore to Westbury and permitting the Bradford to Bathampton cut-off to Bath and Bristol. In 1847 the directors faced problems: loans were unobtainable; calls were not paid and as soon as a call was made the value of the shares dropped almost to the full value of that call. Matters were eased by not letting any new contracts and then reducing or stopping existing works together with delaying the purchase of land. R. P. Brereton was the engineer responsible for constructing the line and it was he who designed most of its stations.

On 21st October, 1847 candidates for the office of secretary were warned that they might suffer a reduction in salary, or be made redundant following the opening of the line. No appointment was made as Saunders, the GWR secretary, asked the WSWR directors to defer filling the position as 'a gentleman of considerable experience' would soon be available for the post. The mystery man was revealed to be Captain William O'Brien who was appointed in December 1847 at a salary of £600 a year. An army officer turned railway administrator, he had been secretary to the Great North of England Railway from 1841 to 1845.

The line from Thingley Junction to Westbury opened on 5th September, 1848, but the remainder of the WSWR was far from complete due to the public not wishing to invest money in the period following the Railway Mania. By the summer of 1848 some land between Westbury and Warminster had yet to be bought, but south of Warminster the principal works had been started. At the half-yearly

> **Wilts, Somerset, and Weymouth Railway.**
> *TENDERS FOR LOANS.*
> THE DIRECTORS of this COMPANY are ready to RECEIVE TENDERS for LOANS, on Security of the Company's Debentures, at 5 per Cent. Interest, payable Half-yearly, for Terms of Three, Five, or Seven Years. Application to be made to the undersigned. W. O'BRIEN, Secretary.
> 449, *West Strand, London.*
> *Trowbridge, Wilts,* 1st February, 1848.
>
> TUESDAY, the 15th day of February inst., to and including TUESDAY, the 29th day of February, inst.
> WALTER LONG, Chairman.
> W. O'BRIEN, Secretary.
> *Trowbridge,* 1st *February,* 1848.

WSWR directors ready to receive tenders for loans. *Wiltshire Independent* 24th February, 1848

meeting of the WSWR on 28th August, 1848 it was announced that a considerable amount of work had been executed between Westbury and Salisbury, but further work had been suspended until that near Westbury was more advanced.

Then on 4th June, 1849 the GWR secretary sent a letter to the WSWR directors saying it was a 'strong and decided' opinion of his directors that steps should be taken to stop all works with the exception of those between Westbury and Frome and arrangements made with contractors so that expenditure would cease on what were considered unproductive portions of the line. On 27th January, 1849 this action led to a meeting being held at Warminster Town Hall and anger expressed at having land taken but no railway built.

In October 1849 the WSWR directors resolved 'that it is highly desirable that the railways authorised by this company should be sold to the Great Western Railway Company upon such terms as will produce to the shareholders in this company, the same rate of interest and other advantages as is provided for them under the agreement between the two companies. This led to a Heads of Agreement between the companies being signed on 31st December, 1849.

During its existence, the WSWR had received £1,264,920 with £235,080 in arrears, making a total of £1½m. There was a total balance of £1,299,509 12s. 4d. (including calls, loans, etc); while payments of £1,264,697 16s. 6d. had been made giving a balance in hand of £34,811 15s. 10d. A final balance of £35,038 15s. 5d. was forwarded to the GWR.

The condition of sale to the GWR was an offer to WSWR shareholders of 4 per cent guaranteed stock in lieu of their ordinary shares, but as the GWR had from the beginning guaranteed 4 per cent, it was only a paper transaction, thus the incomplete WSWR became part of the GWR from 14th March, 1850, Parliament confirming this on 3nd July, 1851 by an Act of 14-15 Vic cap. 48. As soon as the GWR secured the WSWR it immediately set to work finishing the line between Westbury and Warminster. Messrs Barnes & Turner were the contractors, with Rowland Brotherhood making trial borings and holding the permanent way maintenance contract until 1861.

The evening before the single track, broad gauge branch was to be opened as far as Warminster, passengers at Westbury boarding the Warminster bus were given a handbill announcing rustic sports the following day: catching a pig with a greasy tail; climbing a greased pole to win a leg of mutton off the top and donkey racing. In the event, the latter must have lacked excitement as there was only one entry!

The first signs of celebration were at 5.00 am on 9th September, 1851, when cannons sounded from Cop Heap, while somewhat later there was a procession of 1,300 children followed by five or six wagon-loads of children too young to walk yet too old to be left out of the proceedings. Clergy of various denominations also processed to the station accompanied by bands.

Flags flew from churches, bells rang and the station was decorated with evergreens and banners. The *Bristol Times* of 13th September, 1851 was ecstatic:

> Twas no partial festival, carried out in a patch of a place – the whole town rejoiced, from the crown of its head to the sole of its foot – it throbbed with as much emotion as though it felt that England at large had its eye on their proceedings – nay that all Europe, and a part of Asia Minor were observing it.

About 3,000 adult spectators lined up each side of the track to await the arrival of the first train. Quoting the *Bristol Journal*:

> A feather of smoke arose in the distance. "*Advance the broad gauge*" cried a voice and the broad gauge banner was brought a little nearer so that the directors should see, on stepping out, how delicately sensitive Warminster people were; but the broad gauge banner blotted out from view "*Bretheren, dwell together in unity*" against which the bearer of the banner protested, though the incident was not so inappropriate considering the family feuds engendered amongst railway managements by "The Battle of the Gauges"

'Watt' appeared on one of the banners. "'*Tis a mistake*," said one Nonconformist to his wife, "*they've left out the 's'*." "*Oh I see, my love*," was his wife's reply, "*Dr Watts – very proper*," and was very satisfied, believing it a compliment to the man who made the hymns, not the engines!

The first train was hauled into Warminster by *Sagittarius* originally a 2-4-0 goods engine built by Rothwell & Co at Bolton ten years earlier, but subsequently altered to a Leo class 2-4-0ST. As it entered the station the band struck up *The Conquering Hero* and cheers lasted for several minutes. The GWR directors on the train seemed surprised to see such a large crowd to welcome them, only expecting a few flags and a cheer or two.

The 1,400 children dined in their respective schools and then took part in rustic sports, while in a field between the town and the railway a long line of tents filled with a double row of tables and benches offered 400 poor inhabitants aged over 60 a 'substantial dinner' consisting of cold roast beef and plum pudding, washed down with a 'plentiful supply of strong beer'. After riding to Longleat and Shearwater in order to gain an appetite, the directors and others, making a total of 130, dined in the town hall. At this banquet, H. Simonds remarked that he had been

Broad gauge 2-4-0ST *Sagittarius* which worked the first train Westbury–Warminster.

present at the opening of every branch of the Great Western Railway, but at none had he seen 'anything like the cordiality of the magnificent reception of today'. A vocal and instrumental concert was given in the evening, followed by fireworks supplied by Gyngell of Clifton.

Due to shortage of GWR funds, it was not until June 1854, nine years after the Act had been passed for building a line to Salisbury, that Rowland Brotherhood was able to continue his contract to complete the line to that city. As powers granted by the WSWR Act were about to expire, on 31st July, 1854 an Extension of Time Bill was proposed, but opposed by a Meeting of the Salisbury Committee of Landowners. On 25th May, 1854 the GWR directors passed a resolution pledging themselves 'to use their best efforts to ensure the opening of the Line between Salisbury and Warminster for public traffic by 30th June, 1855' providing that the Committee relaxed its opposition which it agreed to do so but reserving ' the right to oppose the Bill in the House of Lords if any situation affecting their interests is made to the Clauses in the Bill in passing through the House of Commons'. Later when efforts to complete the line seemed lacking, the Mayor of Salisbury said that the GWR found it so profitable carrying Bristol to Salisbury passengers via Reading and Basingtoke (another example of 'Great Way Round') that it lacked inducement to complete the direct route. This certainly seemed to be the case and proceedings were taken for a Writ of Mandamus to force the GWR to complete the line, but the railway company's defence was successful.

The 19½ miles from Warminster to Salisbury were able to be built relatively cheaply as no outstanding earthworks were required. Because of their occupation navvies had to be tough men and their work made them thirsty so this combination sometimes led to problems of inappropriate behaviour after drinking too much beer. Most men were living away from home and their parish church, and were likely to feel out of place, so special services were put on for them. On 30th July, 1854 the Revd. Arthur Fane, assisted by Revd. G. Stallard, held a service in the engine shed at Warminster for men employed on the new line, the *Salisbury & Winchester Journal* recording 'The service was well-attended, and the audience conducted themselves with the most complete decorum.' Things were even better on 13th August when the Revd Fane organised a choir of junior choristers to lead the singing and the men were 'grateful for his attention to their spiritual wants'.

A Patriotic Fund was set up to attempt to alleviate the distress suffered by soldiers in the Crimea. The parish of Little Langford collected £4 17s. 2d., £3 12s. 2d. of this being contributed by the navvies attending the evening service on 7th November, 1854 the local paper commenting: 'It was gratifying to notice the readiness with which those railway labourers, who avail themselves of this service, gave their offerings.'

It was all to easy for a contractor to over-reach himself, perhaps having insufficient financial backing, or encountering an unexpected problem, or perhaps material more difficult to excavate than had been anticipated when signing the contract, and so fall into bankruptcy.

In August 1854 Mr Mitchell, a sub-contractor for the Warminster to Salisbury line was decreed bankrupt at the County Court for arrears of wages due to men in his employment, the *Salisbury & Winchester Journal* poignantly commentating:

> Many of these poor fellows were so badly off in consequence of not being paid, that they went about begging from door to door in Warminster. As this is no new occurrence, we think that the attention of the Directors of the Great Western should be called to the matter.

John Mitchell's accounts showed unsecured creditors, chiefly in Wiltshire and Oxfordshire were owed £16,364 6s. 5d. and creditors holding security owed £1,130 15s. 7d. On the credit side, cash at the bankers was £3 14s. 0d.; property surrendered to assignees realised £3,398 6s. 11d.; debtors good and doubtful £58; policies in hands of creditors £44 17s. 0d.; horses sold by creditors realised £270 18s. 3d. while the loss on plant and materials which the GWR claimed to retain because they were on its premises and the contract incomplete were valued abut £6,000. On 26th January, 1856 His Honour said that under the circumstances he would award an immediate certificate of the second class.

Some Salisbury businessmen believed that the GWR station should be in a more central location and on 23nd October, 1854 held a small preliminary meeting prior to discussing the subject with the GWR directors. This resulted in the mayor agreeing to write to Charles Saunders, the company secretary to ascertain whether the GWR could co-operate with the LSWR to build a central station at the cheese market. The directors replied:

> Great Western Railway. London Terminus, Paddington,
> 27th October 1854
>
> Sir – I have had the honour to receive your letter of the 24th inst., which has been submitted to the Board of Directors for their consideration.
>
> I am desired by them to acquaint you that there appears to be no Parliamentary authority for the construction of any such station in Salisbury as is adverted to in your letter; and that considerable delay would be occasioned in the progress and completion of the Railway between Warminster and Salisbury by any alteration of the plans already sanctioned by Parliament, and in the course of construction.
>
> The Directors do not feel justified at present in embarking in any new project involving additional expenditure beyond that which has been rendered obligatory on them by existing acts.
>
> If hereafter it shall appear advantageous to the inhabitants of Salisbury to convert the separate termini of Railways in their city into a through line, with one common terminus, so as to have all traffic carried forward without passing into the streets, or giving the opportunity of trade to the hotels or shops, usually enriched in a terminal town, it may certainly be attended with public advantage, and confer a benefit on the Railway companies.
>
> If such a costly work be undertaken by others, the Directors may be glad to avail themselves of it to any extent found necessary, upon equitable conditions.
>
> I have the honour to be Sir, your obedient Servant,
>   Chas. A. Saunders, Secretary.
> To the Worshipful the Mayor of Salisbury.

It was a very clever letter suggesting that the status quo was best and throwing the ball into their court,

Railway construction was a dangerous occupation with the ever-present risk of rock or earth falls, or being struck by earth-moving wagons. Tunnel construction was the most hazardous, but there were no tunnels on this length of line. On 22nd November, 1854 a fall of earth at

FIRST PROPOSALS

Langford buried a navvy up to his chest. He was immediately extricated and conveyed to Salisbury Infirmary where he had been an inmate two months previously when his leg had been broken in the same manner.

On 26th June, 1855 James Thring, working in the parish of Langford fell from a tip wagon down an embankment dislocating his collar bone. Taken to Salisbury Infirmary it was reported four days later than he was 'progressing favourably'.

In February 1856 Alderman Kelsey said that the time had arrived when, in his opinion the council was fully justified in moving that the town clerk be instructed to write to the GWR reminding them of their pledge long since made that the Warminster to Salisbury line would be open to traffic by last July and requesting to be informed when it would be open. As this pledge had been given under the seal of the company on condition that an opposition should be withdrawn. The town clerk received the reply;

> Great Western Railway, London Terminus, Paddington
> 28th April 1856

> Sir, – In reply to your letter of 23rd inst., the directors desire me to state they hope to complete the line between Salisbury and Warminster in July.
>   I remain, Sir, your obedient Servant,
>   Charles Saunders, Secretary.

The single broad gauge line was opened to mineral traffic on 11th June, 1856, giving impetus to the coal trade at Radstock, all pits there connected with the GWR having more orders than could be fulfilled. On 17th June, 1856 the Board of Trade inspector, Colonel Yolland, together with Ward, the residential engineer, accompanied by several Great Western officials together with, surprisingly, 'a number of ladies', inspected the line. The *Salisbury & Winchester Journal* of 19th June, 1856 recorded

> On the arrival of the train at the Salisbury Terminus they were loudly cheered by several hundred persons in waiting. After partaking of an elegant luncheon, laid out at the Terminus by Mr. Jones, of the White Hart, the party returned to the train, and left at five o'clock pm. We are informed that the inspection was in every respect highly satisfactory and that the line will very shortly be permanently opened for traffic.

The full opening was to be on 1st July, 1856, but the Mayor of Salisbury with a view to making the holiday appointed to commemorate the anniversary of the Coronation of Queen Victoria more interesting, persuaded the directors to open the line to passengers on 30th June, 1856. Due to shortage of time for preparations it went ahead without many of the usual formalities which the Victorians so enjoyed, though the first Up train which left Salisbury at 6.40 am on 30th June, 1856 was decorated with flowers and evergreens, a large crowd witnessing its departure. London was now 136.3 miles from Salisbury via Swindon, Chippenham and Westbury, or 95.6 miles via Eastleigh, but when the direct line to Waterloo via Andover was opened it reduced the London & South Western distance to 83.8 miles, while the Lavington cut-off brought that of the GWR down to 121.1 miles.

The first Down train arrived at 11.00 am 'a very large number of persons being assembled at the Station' and most of the five trains each way were noted as well-filled. At some of the stations flags were displayed. From Warminster, stations on the opening day were at Heytesbury, Codford, Wiley (this spelling lasted until 1874), Langford (only open for about 16 months), Wishford, Wilton and Salisbury: all were designed by R. P. Brereton.

The *Salisbury & Winchester Journal* of 5th July, 1856 recorded:

> In consequence of the length of time which has been occupied in its construction, it is now consolidated, and this, together with the peculiar mode of laying rails on the Great Western line, causes the propulsion of the train to be unattended with that oscillation which is so unpleasant on some of the narrow gauge lines. It passes through a valley remarkable for fertility, and the diversity of its scenery in parts of the line is remarkably picturesque.

The *Salisbury & Winchester Journal* continued:

> The opening of this line will be the means of bringing the extensive coal fields of Somersetshire into closer proximity with this city, and also with the important port of Southampton and the great naval arsenal of Portsmouth in which such places, for a long time past, prices have ranged high in consequence of the great demand for coals for the purposes of steam navigation.
>
> The terminus, which is within half a mile of the Cathedral, is well-constructed, being in fact an ornament to the place; and the other stations on the line are substantial buildings, well-constructed, and of suitable dimensions for a large amount of traffic. The line has been opened just a month earlier than the time stipulated by Act of Parliament....On the whole we have little doubt that the opening of the line to this city will be productive of great advantages to the inhabitants of this locality.

Brake vans used on the WSWR were originally formed from passenger luggage vans 22 feet by 8 feet, divided into six compartments, the guard's in the centre. The wheels pierced the floor and were protected by an iron casing. These vans were constructed from iron plates and angle iron. Their brakes were efficient and could hold a heavy goods train on Scudamore Bank. Until *circa* 1870 they were used on both passenger and goods trains, but around that year oak vans were used on the former with a window and brake handle at each end; later these vans had bay windows and were painted to match passenger stock.

At first tilt, or the alternative name of bonnet, wagons were used for almost all classes of goods traffic. Of wrought-iron plating they measured 17 feet by 9 feet 8 inches with a height floor to crown of 7 feet 8 inches, they were latterly used just for coal; in 1874 some were converted for use on the standard gauge.

In 1857 the GWR made an unsuccessful attempt to promote a broad gauge extension from Salisbury to Southampton to be known as the Southampton, Bristol & South Wales Railway, which would have crossed the LSWR on a viaduct.

In 1870 the GWR had made an agreement between the standard gauge Bristol & North Somerset Railway (which connected Bristol and

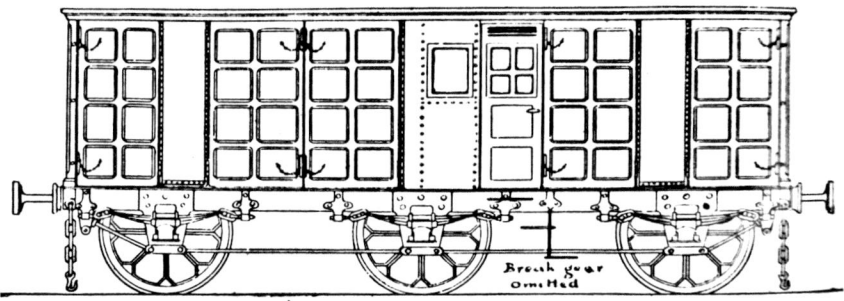

Six-wheeled broad gauge brake van of circa 1860.

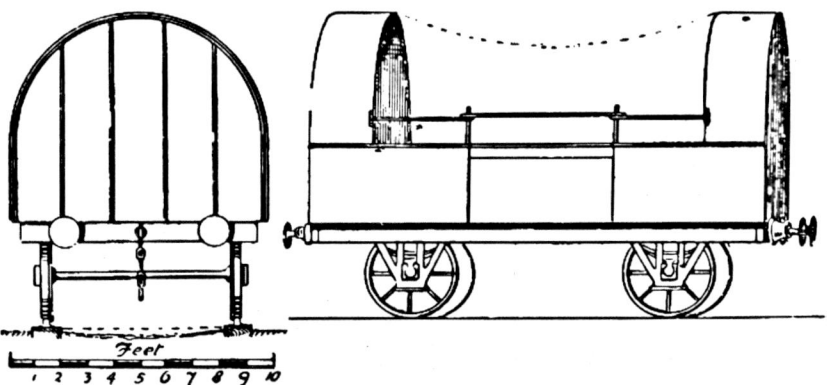

GWR broad gauge 'bonnet' wagon used for traffic on WSWR.

Westbury view Down in broad gauge days: the train shed is on the left and Westbury Iron Works in the background. *Author's collection*

Radstock), and the colliery owners to provide standard gauge between Radstock and Salisbury, on or before February 1875, so in February 1874 the GWR directors announced that gauge conversion would take place that year. To facilitate this, no trains ran between Westbury and Salisbury on 19th-21st June, while on 16th-18th, 22nd and 23nd June and until further notice, the regular service was suspended, but four trains each way would run – from Salisbury for Bristol and intermediate stations at 6.30 am, 9.45 am, 2.00 pm and 5.30 pm. Similarly trains from Bristol to Salisbury and intermediate stations would leave at 5.15 am, 11.45 am, 1.30 pm and 5.00 pm.

Conversion to standard gauge was carried out in the usual highly-efficient manner. The track was prepared for slewing to the standard gauge by clearing away the ballast and marking the transoms where they should be cut. These were set every 11 feet and each alternate one had been disconnected and partly sawn to the standard gauge length and all nuts and bolts had been oiled to effect quick removal. Substitute short rails were provided at curves to avoid wasting time cutting the outer rail when moved inwards. Armies of platelayers and their equipment were brought by special train to begin preparations early on Tuesday 16th June, 1874.

Late in the evening of Thursday 18th June, 1874, all broad gauge vehicles were removed from the branch and engines took the precaution of taking water at every possible point so that should they become derailed through the looseness of the permanent way due to the bolts

Great Western Railway
LOCOMOTIVE DEPARTMENT.

CONVERSION OF GAUGE
BETWEEN THINGLEY JUNCTION & DORCHESTER,
Including the Salisbury, Bathampton, Radstock, Wells, and Bridport Branches.

NOTICE TO ENGINEMEN AND FIREMEN.

Every Engineman working over the above-mentioned Lines, during the Conversion of the Gauge, will be supplied with a copy of the printed TIME TABLE AND GENERAL INSTRUCTIONS issued for the use of the Company's Servants, for which his signature will be taken. No Engineman must on any account take charge of an Engine or Train on any part of these Lines or Branches after Monday, 15th June, or subsequently during the Conversion, who has not previously received and signed for, the Time Table and General Instructions.

The Enginemen are requested to make themselves thoroughly acquainted with the Time Bill and General Instructions, and they will be expected to read them through with great care as soon as they receive them, and if they meet with anything which they do not properly understand, or which they think requires explanation, they must at once apply to their Superintendent, or Foreman, or one of the Locomotive Inspectors on duty, in order that there may be no misunderstanding whatever on the part of the men engaged in this work.

The particular attention of the Enginemen is directed to clause 15 of the General Instructions on Page 12 as to stopping "*dead*" at the end of each Section; also to Clause 47, Page 15. ALL FACING POINTS MUST BE APPROACHED WITH VERY GREAT CAUTION, and at the Crossing Places the greatest care must be taken to have the Engine or Train so under control, as to prevent the possibility of overshooting the Points.

Enginemen and Firemen must keep a constant look out for any signal that may be given by the Permanent Way Men or others, whether by means of a Red Flag or other Hand-signal: They are to proceed with great caution, especially on approaching curves, when they must take care to sound their small whistles, so as to give timely warning of their approach to the men working on the Line.

Enginemen and Firemen are particularly requested to be with their Engines in good time, and to bestow the greatest care upon the oiling and examination of the working parts, Axle Boxes, &c. They must be particularly careful to have a good supply of coal before starting from each end, and to fill up their tanks at every watering place, so as to be fully prepared for any unexpected stoppage or delay. So much depends upon the Engines being in the best possible working order, that it is hoped very great attention will be paid to this matter, MORE ESPECIALLY WITH THE NEW NARROW GAUGE ENGINES.

Firemen are also required to make themselves well acquainted with the Time Table and General Instructions, and the Enginemen must afford them every opportunity of doing so. As far as possible the Enginemen and Firemen should read the instructions TOGETHER, so as to obtain a perfect knowledge of them before commencing to work the single line.

J. ARMSTRONG.

Engineer's Office, Swindon.
    13th June, 1874.

Notice to enginemen and firemen re conversion of gauge, 1874.

being eased beforehand, they would not run out of water before being re-railed.

At 3.00 am on 19th June the slewing of the longitudinal sleepers began in typical warm, dry June weather. The *Bath & Cheltenham Gazette* of 24th June, 1874 recorded:

> Nearly 2,000 men were employed (this included all the Wilts, Somerset & Weymouth Railway), each receiving 1*s*. 3*d*. per day extra in addition to his usual wages of 4*s*. 6*d*. The men worked the whole of the 18 hours during which daylight now exists. Lodging accommodation was provided by the Company where it could not be obtained in the places through which the line passes. The Company supplied the men with oatmeal, sugar and pure water. The work having been completed by the appointed time, the officials of the Company were busily employed on Sunday in conveying narrow gauge stock from Swindon to Salisbury, Weymouth, Bristol &c.

On Sunday 21st June the mostly new standard gauge trains proceeded to Salisbury at walking pace driven by the Salisbury men who had worked the broad gauge stock to Swindon and partial services were operated. The first standard gauge train from Salisbury to Bristol was headed by Dean 2-4-0 Metro tank No. 615, followed by No. 632 of the same class. The cost of narrowing the gauge was estimated to be £290,000, this including necessary alterations to stations and other works; although to some extent provision had been made for the supply of standard gauge rolling stock, a further outlay of £70,000 was needed to cover the cost of locomotives, carriages and wagons necessary to work the traffic.

At first the only crossing loop was at Wylye, but a loop opened at Wilton in 1867, double track was opened between Westbury and Warminster in May 1875 largely to ease the return of banking engines; loops were opened at Heytesbury 4th March, 1877; Codford 5th February, 1877 and Wishford in August 1896, but traffic on the line developed to such an extent that doubling was the only answer. Wilton to Salisbury was doubled 1st July, 1896; the 2¼ mile section from Heytesbury through Upton Lovell to Codford in 1899 and the continuation of this through Sherrington to Wylye, 3¼ miles distant achieved on 13th January, 1900. Warminster to Heytesbury was doubled in October 1900, while on 10th December, 1900 a new box at Upton Scudamore was opened with a siding facility for bankers and also a crossover. Wylye to Wishford was doubled 3rd March, 1901; Wishford to Wilton 28th April, 1901. The entire 24¼ miles from Westbury to Salisbury was now entirely double-tracked. Bunker coal was by now a very important traffic as by 1907 a large Atlantic liner would burn 1,000 tons of coal every 24 hours.

The real benefit of the change of gauge came about in August 1877 when it was agreed that a connecting line could be laid at Salisbury between the GWR and the LSWR. Ultimately it was this link that was the driving force behind turning the Salisbury branch into a double-track main line. It was now possible to run through trains from South Wales to Southampton for filling the bunkers of merchant ships and those of the Royal Navy at Portsmouth. Routing of this traffic became even easier with the opening of the Severn Tunnel to goods on 1st September, 1886.

In 1881 snow caused the line between Westbury and Salisbury to be blocked from the afternoon of Tuesday 18th January. In the evening, as the 2.00 pm Bristol to Salisbury train had not arrived at Warminster, that station sent a telegram to Westbury and received a reply that it had left at the usual time. When a further message was received that the train was held in a drift at the summit of Scudamore Bank, a gang of men was sent from Warminster. It transpired from the guard that his train had left Westbury at 4.08 pm after waiting for the connection from Swindon which failed to arrive. His train had two engines which struck snow in the cutting at the head of Scudamore Bank, the 30 passengers shaken as it suddenly stopped. The snow was as high as his van's windows and on leaving the train he was immediately up to his neck in a drift..

A messenger was sent on to Warminster, reaching the station with difficulty as in places the snow was waist-deep. About 5.30 pm the rescue gang from Warminster arrived at the marooned train, but due to the wind causing drifting, any space they cleared was quickly filled. Realising work was useless, they sought shelter in the guard's van and some of the carriages. At 10.00 pm when conditions had somewhat eased, they set to work. The passengers had been without relief or refreshments for four to five hours until Mr Young, the Warminster station master appeared with a bottle of brandy and a few biscuits; a Mr J. Scott also sent plenty of refreshments to the stranded travellers. At about midnight enough snow had been cleared to allow passengers to leave the carriages and just a single coach, van and an engine took them on to Warminster station. Most remained at the station all night, one woman with four children sleeping in the porters' room and the others in the waiting room. H. P. Jones, steward to the Marquis of Bath, seeing children shaking with cold, had them and their mother taken to an hotel in the town.

Next day men were at work clearing the summit cutting, but the wind filled it again. The men struck for pay at 10*s*. 0*d*. a day which was granted. By noon on 20th January it was possible to run an engine on the Up line from Warminster to Westbury. That afternoon a special train conveyed passengers to Westbury with the intention of reaching Salisbury via Yeovil, but finding the Yeovil line blocked, they were returned to Warminster. The 2.00 pm Bristol to Salisbury service of 18th January eventually reached Salisbury on the evening of 21st January, while the Swindon goods, embedded in a drift between Heytesbury and Codford on 18th January, failed to arrive at Salisbury until 2.00 pm on 22nd January. Warminster inhabitants were unable, except by telegraph, to communicate with anyone outside the town from Tuesday evening until Thursday afternoon, the *Salisbury & Wimborne Journal* stating that its report had been telegraphed.

As to events on the rest of the branch, no GWR train left Salisbury after 1.15 pm on Tuesday 18th January. On Friday a train with two engines, two coaches and a van left Salisbury for Warminster at 3.55 pm reaching its destination and that same evening a train arrived from Bristol.

The line suffered similarly in the Great Blizzard of March 1891. Snow began to fall shortly after 2.00 pm on Monday 9th March and increased in intensity as the day advanced. A strong east wind blew and by Tuesday morning the snow was several inches thick and several feet deep where it had drifted. No irregularity to the train service was experienced until the cattle train from Taunton left Westbury at about 1.00 am on Tuesday but after struggling through the snow, ran into a huge drift at Biss Bottom Cutting from which it tried to extricate itself but remained immovable. One of the guards went on to Westbury and returned with Mr Martin, the station master, a gang of men and an engine. By this time the whole train was embedded in snow and the wagons had to be dug out individually. Eventually the two engines succeeded in hauling the train back to Westbury where the wagons were covered with tarpaulins to protect the sheep and cattle from the weather and they were fed with hay.

Early that morning an empty mineral train from Salisbury to Aberdare was caught in a drift on the Warminster side of Codford station, but with the assistance of another engine was able to proceed to Heytesbury where it was shunted into a siding where it remained until Wednesday afternoon. A passenger train left Salisbury at 1.05 pm and with great difficulty reached Warminster at 3.45 pm on Tuesday, but due to a snowdrift at Biss Bottom could not proceed, its passengers lodging in the town overnight. Unfortunately a woman and two children were unprepared for the contingency and had no money for accommodation.

An early drawing of the south side of Warminster station: the train shed is beyond the offices; a horse bus awaits passengers. The goods shed stands on the far right with a bonnet wagon between the two buildings.
Author's collection

The original GWR Salisbury shed circa 1898: 0-6-0ST on the turntable. Beyond is the water tank with a coaling platform below with the sand furnace and its tall chimney to the left. Two point levers can also be seen on the left. An LSWR tender is on the far right with the LSWR passenger station beyond. All the GWR rail is flat-bottomed, but that of the LSWR is bull-head.
Author's collection

A kind gentleman took them to the Magnet for lodgings while eight male passengers spent the night in the waiting room. All left at noon on Wednesday.

On Tuesday it was hoped that the morning train would be able to get through to Salisbury. Instead of arriving at 10.52 am it arrived at 1.00 pm. Three passengers who had missed the passenger train at Westbury were permitted to travel in the guard's van of a Down cattle train and when it struck the snowdrift at Biss Bottom and suddenly stopped, they were thrown from their seats. To prevent himself falling one passenger hugged the stove pipe which was nearly red hot, the second was pitched to the floor, and the third passenger turned the brake handle the wrong way. It was found that the brake van and last wagon had been running derailed for about a mile but they had been unaware of this until they reached a spot where the wind had swept the rail clear of snow. The derailment damaged the track. The cattle were fed, the vehicles re-railed and the train run to Warminster where it remained until Wednesday afternoon but damage to the Down line was not repaired until Thursday afternoon.

An inspector and the assistant superintendent of the district with two engines tried on Tuesday afternoon to force a passage to Salisbury but could get no further than Heytesbury where they were forced to remain for the night. On Wednesday morning two engines and a snow plough thrust their way from Salisbury to Heytesbury where they were coupled to the two engines which had spent the night there, the four locomotives then proceeding to Westbury. The drifts in some places were as high as the tenders, that near Codford station being the deepest. On their return to Warminster about midday, the passenger train which had been detained all night was despatched. As the driver of the Warminster to Bath mail cart was stopped by a drift on Monday evening and unable to get through, the letters remained at Warminster until noon on Wednesday when they were sent by rail.

A contributor to the *Western Daily Press* of 12th March, 1891 who had been a passenger in that train held overnight at Warminster wrote:

> On Tuesday I secured a seat in the 1.05 pm train from Salisbury for Warminster. I was told that, although this should have been the third, it was really the first train of the day. Matters went on all right until we reached Wylye, a small village about ten miles from Salisbury. Here occurred a somewhat unusual delay, the line to be traversed being a single one, on which a snow plough was at work, and until its arrival we could go no further.
>
> We were detained there the best part of an hour, and to create a diversion, one of us proposed that we should alight and investigate affairs, and ascertain the prospects of a move. Neither guard nor driver could give us the

information we wanted, but in answer to further inquiries, the next best thing was to go to the village to get some refreshment.

We conveyed the welcome news to our friends in our compartment. Some joined us. Others, gentlemen of more years and less agility, elected to stay, but in response to an offer from one of our number, expressed a wish that we would bring something back with us.

In a few seconds three or four of us were scampering across the line, up a steep embankment, through a bank of snow almost reaching our knees, where hands had to do their share in locomotion, over a line of wooden rails, and thence into the main road leading to the village inn. We passed several returning parties who had the start of us, and found the house in a state of commotion, the landlord taxed to the limit of his resources to supply the sudden and unusual influx of customers.

Having satisfied our own personal wants, and secured the necessary refreshments for our friends in the train, we returned with as much haste as possible, knowing that on the arrival of the engine for which we were waiting, there would be little further delay of our own departure, but there was little need for haste, for a good hour and a half had elapsed ere the plough came in sight and we moved on.

An Irishman in the compartment produced a flask of spirits and a plentiful supply of eatables from his pockets, which, with true Hibernian generosity, he offered to freely distribute among us.

The scene through which we passed excited our interest and admiration. A white wall of snow was thrown up on each side of us. Here it was just above the footboards of the carriage. A little further on, where the drift had been deeper, it reached up to the windows, while now and then, for stretches of 100 yards or so, where the cutting was deepest, the ridges of the banks were crested with thick piles of snow that overhung like the eaves of a roof, shaking with the vibration of the air, and occasionally breaking away and sliding down the bank like a miniature avalanche.

Creeping cautiously along, we passed through Codford and Heytesbury, and at length reached Warminster, and here another long stoppage was made to await the arrival of a train from Westbury. That something unusual had occurred was evident by the arrival of a few luggage vans, drawn by three engines, and our anxiety was increased by the consultations between the guards and the local officials.

Personal inquiries led to nothing immediately definite, but after some time spent in wiring to headquarters and awaiting replies, the facts came out. One line of rails between ourselves and Westbury was blocked by an impassable barrier of snow, which it was impossible to clear that night. On the other line traffic was rendered impossible owing to the displacement of sleepers for a considerable distance. This was caused by the rear van of the train just arrived having left the rails, and the triple power in front dragged it bumping and thumping, for some distance before the mishap was noticed, and the van disconnected.

Up to this time we had regarded our difficulties as of a passing, if unpleasant, character; but the prospect of a forced stay for the night was too serious to be regarded lightly. There were a few women and children in the

Ex-Bristol & Exeter Railway 2-4-0 No. 3 at Salisbury as GWR No. 1355. Built in 1874 it was withdrawn in 1883. The hinged block in the foreground prevents an unauthorised movement.
D. W. Churchill

Nemesis a broad gauge Standard Goods engine at Warminster 1874 just prior to the change of gauge. This engine was withdrawn in November 1877. *Author's collection*

train ill provided with means to defray the expenses of a night from home. It was long past the time when we should have arrived at Bristol and the little ones were crying with cold and hunger.

I think under the circumstances the station-master should be empowered to act on his own responsibility and judgment in relieving the immediate necessities of poor belated travellers; but beyond the intimation that the waiting-room and fire was at their disposal, nothing was done. A couple of us went down to the town with a view to making some arrangements for the weaker folks. The prospect of a night in the waiting-room for these little ones was one we did not care to contemplate. The proprietor of a coffee house expressed his willingness to accommodate the women and children at a minimum charge, but before we had quite concluded the negotiations a gentleman, who had some connection with a Railway Travellers' Aid Society, made his appearance and with his co-operation the matter was finally arranged.

Hotels were crowded, beds all engaged, and a few of the most unselfish found themselves unprovided for. Six or seven of the rough and ready passengers had made things as comfortable as possible in the waiting-room, where a good fire had been provided. When things were looking desperately bad, I managed to secure a bed in the house of a tradesman, to whom I feel under an obligation far beyond the modest amount he deigned to accept. After a hearty meal I rejoined some of my friends, who had expressed a kindly anxiety on my account.

Next morning the uncertainty of the time of our departure necessitated frequent visits to the station, and return visits to the various hostelries where we had slept, and at last, somewhere between 11 and 12 o'clock, after weary watching and waiting, our train really did start. From then on trains ran normally.

The railway at Westbury was more sheltered and there was no trouble from drifting. On Tuesday evening a few passengers destined for Salisbury were detained overnight at Westbury as their train could not proceed further. Mr Martin, the station master, provided lodgings for the two lady passengers and the gentlemen were made comfortable in the waiting room.

In 1895 the War Department purchased a large tract of Salisbury Plain for military training, this, of course bringing extra traffic to the Westbury–Salisbury line. The First World War and the use of the Plain for military purposes, saw further development of the line, new sidings and loading platforms being constructed at Westbury, Warminster, Heytesbury, Codford, Wylye and Wishford. At Codford a new military platform and sidings were ready for use in October 1914. The Codford Camp Railway and the Sutton Veny Camp Railway built by the War Department were operated by them until May 1918 when the GWR took over working.

The military traffic meant that a great number of trains were received and despatched in the area. For example in July 1916 the movement of the 60th (London) Division from camps near Warminster, Heytesbury and Codford to Southampton involved running no less than 88 special trains from these stations. Similarly the line carried extra military traffic in Second World War, tank loading platforms being brought into use at Warminster in 1939.

When William Peter Hamilton, British born editor of the *Wall Street Journal* visited England in 1923, Sir Felix Pole, the general manager of the GWR, was one of the first people he met. Mentioning that he would be visiting his sister who lived near Salisbury, Sir Felix said: '*All right, I'll see you're treated like visiting royalty on my line.*' 'Thanks,' said Hamilton, '*but isn't your Salisbury line a great way round?*' '*It is,*' agreed Sir Felix, '*but **I'm** giving you a Great Western general pass!*'

With Nationalisation coming into effect on 1st January, 1948, initially the line became part of the Western Region, but on 2nd April, 1950 was transferred to the Southern Region. Train services remained unaltered, but civil engineering staff and signalling and telegraph staff came under the new management. It was one of the first main lines on British Railways to suffer the widespread closure of stations, when all those between Warminster and Salisbury were shut to passengers on 19th September, 1955. In 1970 the Bristol to Salisbury line was given a three-year grant of £110,000 per annum.

As a Sprinter approached Salisbury in September 1995 a buzzard swooped over into its path and got its head caught in a fuel tank. It was not discovered until the train reached Portsmouth Harbour. There the station staff freed it and took it to Brent Lodge Wildlife Hospital at Sidlesham near Chichester where it was treated for a broken wing.

Chapter Two

The Bristol, South Wales & Southampton Union Railway

An interesting proposal suggested by the imminent opening of the Westbury–Salisbury line was the Bristol & South Wales Union Railway. The idea was raised at a meeting in Bristol on 31st October, 1854 when it was suggested that links should be improved to South Wales as rail distances were 82 miles to Newport and 93 to Cardiff whereas the direct distances were 20 and 26 miles respectively.

Thomas Evans Blackwall, engineer to the proposed line, had visited Scotland and witnessed the working of steam floating bridges – in other words steam ferries – across the firths Forth and Tay and believed one would be possible across the Severn. He said that 200 tons of coal could be carried on each passage and that eight trips could be made daily. A line would be laid to New Passage where a pier would be built and a train shunted onto a ferry which would cross to Portskewett where at another pier the coaches and wagons would be hauled off and drawn along a short branch to join the South Wales Railway.

Blackwall reported that a responsible contractor had agreed to build the line for £600,000. The estimated passenger revenue was £23,164 and total revenue for passengers, goods and merchandise placed at £43,817, equal to a dividend of over 7¼ per cent.

Government support for a railway was unusual, but the following was received by Mr Havenhill of Warminster:

War Office October 28, 1854

My Dear Mr Havenhill,
The plan of the Proposed Bristol, South Wales & Southampton Railway has been before me and also before Lord Hardinge and the Quarter master-general. To consider that the proposed line would be of great value as a shortening by so many miles the distance between Pembroke and South Wales on the one side, and Plymouth, Devonport and Portsmouth on the other; and the Military department will give the line all the support they can command.
Believe me, yours truly,

(Signed) Sidney Herbert

The authorising Act was passed on 27th July, 1857, Rowland Brotherhood starting the contract in October 1858. Like other contractors, he used locomotives to carry spoil from cuttings to make embankments and these engines had to be moved across country between various contracts. His son Peter designed a locomotive capable of travelling on road or railway and in 1862 one of these 11-ton machines

The Bristol, South Wales & Southampton Union Railway pier at New Passage.
Oakwood Press

travelled from his headquarters at Chippenham to the Bristol & South Wales Railway at Patchway over ordinary roads at an average speed of 6 mph.

Due to the great difference in levels between high and low tide – three times that of the Forth or Tay, a rail link between pier and ferry would have been an expensive problem to solve so the train ferry idea was abandoned and the cheaper stairs or hydraulic lifts to pontoons for just foot passengers adopted.

The line was ceremonially opened on 25th August, 1863, public opening being 8th September, 1863, the line worked by the GWR. Just carrying passengers, it would have had little impact on Westbury–Salisbury traffic. It is interesting to record that Charles Richardson, a pupil of I. K. Brunel while engaged on building the piers, was led to consider the project of cutting the Severn Tunnel which definitely did increase Westbury–Salisbury traffic.

Chapter Three

Salisbury Market House Railway

A Salisbury line which should be mentioned as the GWR supplied it with traffic, is the Salisbury Railway & Market House Company which received authorisation on 14th July, 1856. The preamble to its Act stated 'The Market Place at Salisbury is at a considerable distance from the several Railway Stations and the means of communication between the Market Place and these Railways are incommodious'. Initially it was intended to have a street tramway between the LSWR and the market, but as this would have interfered with road traffic an independent line was preferred. This was 2 furlongs 70 yards in length from a junction with the LSWR east of its station running to the west side of the Market Place where the company was empowered to build 'a Market House with stores and all suitable works and conveniences'. The authorised capital was £12,000 increased by £5,000 in 1864 by a second Act, borrowing powers being £3,600 increased by £1000 in 1864. The first Act stipulated that the LSWR should make the railway and maintain the line to ensure that 'the safe and uninterrupted passage along the same should not be impaired' although the cost was to be borne by the Salisbury Railway & Market House Company.

   The line was built by Thomas Brassey at a cost of £1,401 8*s.* 8*d*. The Market House Company's engineer was John Strapp and in that short length a viaduct had two 12 feet openings, a second stream was crossed by another 12 feet span; the River Avon crossed by a 20 feet span and finally a bridge of 30 feet span over the Mill Leat. Then in 1857 the Basingstoke & Salisbury and the Salisbury & Yeovil railways amalgamated, this causing the level of the line to be altered and thus causing the works of the Market House Railway to be abandoned with no compensation. The Market House Company petitioned against the amalgamation of the Basingstoke and Yeovil lines, succeeded in obtaining amending clauses for the LSWR to install within two years the Market House Railway at the original estimated cost and provide a tunnel under its line to permit a broad gauge link with the GWR. In the event, a broad gauge link was never made. The line was on a gradient of 1 in 60 falling from the junction with the LSWR. To guard against runaways, catch points were in abundance.

   The steelwork of the Market House roof and galleries was erected by Messrs W. Mahon of Ardwick, Manchester and shortly after completion the supporting girders failed due to their inadequate design. Eventually the engineer Strapp agreed to refund £550 before the matter came to Court.

The Market House and its railway opened on 24th May, 1859 with a celebratory dinner followed by a concert given by the Band of the 1st Battalion of the City of Salisbury Rifle Corps. The building cost £2,887, measured 77 feet by 174 feet with walls of red and white brick and a glass roof; its pedimented facade was of Bath stone. Provision was made for installing a clock to be given by the mayor if the building was completed during his term of office.

A gallery was provided for storing corn two sacks deep. Despite its name, the market railway never carried meat, fish and poultry as was originally envisaged and within nine months of opening cheese, corn and wool, with which commodities the building principally dealt, occupied all the available space. Cheese traffic ceased in 1903, corn in 1913 and by 1918 traffic into the actual market building was so light that the maintenance of the track in the building could not be justified and so was lifted. Seasonal wool traffic lasted until 1940 when only the corn traffic remained. In 1953 the galleries were leased to Dunn's seeds. Latterly the line was mainly concerned with transporting coal and barley to the maltings which had grown up on each side of the line, sawmills also providing traffic. In the period following the Second World War, coal for the Salisbury Electric Light & Supply Company, later part of the Southern Electricity Board, formed the principal traffic but this ceased when the power station changed to oil fuel in 1962.

The line was leased by the LSWR for £225 per annum, the rental being reduced to £112 11s. 0d. by 1896. The Market House Railway Company paid its first dividend, 3½ per cent, in 1866 and subsequently 5 per cent was paid quite frequently until 1895 when revenue started to decline. Despite the reduction of traffic the company continued to pay respectable dividends – 5½ per cent in 1933 and 12½ per cent in the 1950s. Latterly British Railways managed and worked the line at an annual rent of £150 – £10 less than the LSWR charged 90 years previously!

In BR days 'All classes of locomotives except A1/X, B4, M7, O2, 700 and 0298 were prohibited from working the Market House sidings'. Staff could recall Class G6 and 0395 0-6-0Ts and Class 415 4-4-2Ts working the line and the steepness of the gradients was such, 1 in 60 falling from a junction with the LSWR, that a load of even 20 tons could cause the loss of adhesion.

Following the line's closure on 1st July, 1964, track was lifted that December and the company wound up by voluntary liquidation in 1965. The facade of the Market House building remains, and the public library now occupies the site.

Chapter Four

Description of the Line

Westbury station (109 miles 63 chains from Paddington via Swindon) opened on 5th September, 1848 as the temporary terminus of the first section of the Wilts, Somerset & Weymouth Railway. Designed by J. Geddes, the station was a typical Brunelian timber structure, its overall roof covering two platforms – each only five feet in width – and similar to the extant Frome station. It is believed that an island platform was inserted between the two existing platforms between 1852 and 1855. Westbury was the station where the Weymouth and Salisbury branches divided. When the Patney & Chirton to Westbury cut-off was opened 29th July, 1900 it then placed the station on the main line between Paddington and Plymouth.

In preparation for the opening of this shorter route between Reading and Taunton, in 1899 the original structure at Westbury was replaced by two 600 feet long island platforms reached by subway from the main station building set at ground level and to facilitate transfer of luggage to the platforms on the first floor, lifts were provided. In 1899 Paddington had designed a simpler form of column to support a roof canopy and one of its first appearances was at Westbury. A channel-

Westbury, view Down: a 0-6-0PT stands at the platform with an Up goods and its fireman probably talking to the signalman at Westbury North. *Author's collection*

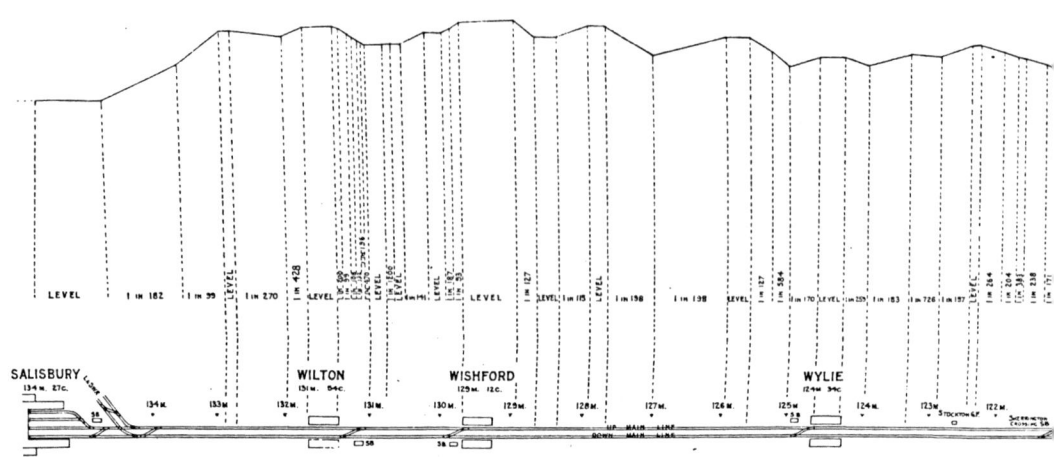

Gradient profile and station plans.

An open-backed Metro class 2-4-0T at Westbury in 1908. To the right is what is probably a 0-6-0ST. *A. Church collection*

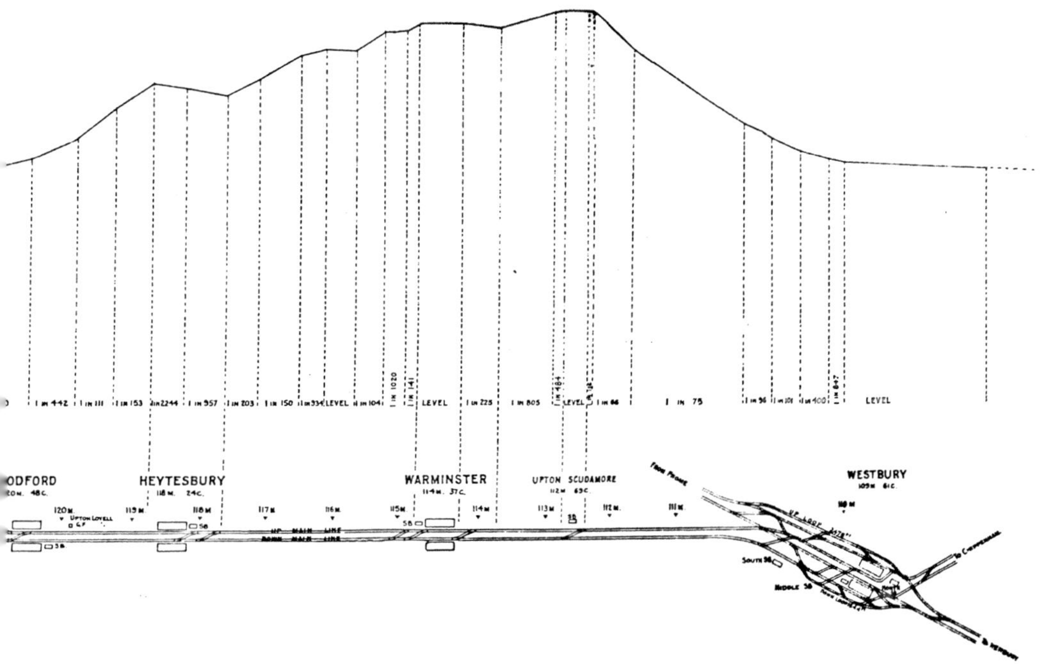

DESCRIPTION OF THE LINE

Westbury, view Up towards the passenger station with Westbury Iron Works on the left and goods shed centre right. The distant signal arms are red indicating that the image was taken before 1927. *Author's collection*

shaped column was built from angled steel with wide webs riveted to flat steel uprights. Across the top of the column a steel beam extended from eave to eave of the awning and in the angle formed between the upright and the crosspiece an ornate bracket was fixed. Platform 1 was the Down Salisbury; Platform 2 the Down Main; Platform 3 the Up Salisbury and Platform 4 the Up Main. In 1978 Platform 1 was taken out of use, so the former Platform 2 was renumbered 1, 3 became 2 and 4 became 3, these three roads being signalled for bi-directional use.

Two brick structures on the Up island platform contained gentlemen's toilets, a porters' office, a general waiting room, a ladies' waiting room, ladies' toilets and an office. On the Down side five brick buildings housed gentlemen's toilets, the telegraph office, station master's office, inspector's office, third class ladies' waiting room, first class ladies' waiting room, ladies' toilets, third class general waiting room, first class general waiting room and a refreshment room.

South-east of the passenger station was the divisional superintendent's office, the blacksmith's shop, stores, the carpenter's shop, the plumber and painter's building and a further store. Between the superintendent's office and the shops were carriage sidings: one of 395 feet and the other 339 feet.

For goods traffic, an 83 feet long shed was provided with a 150 feet loading platform and extensive nearby sidings. The shed had 30 cwt crane with a radius of 12 feet, while near the passenger station was a 12 ton double and 6 ton single crane with a radius of 18 feet. Westbury was able to deal with the whole range of goods traffic including wheeled vehicles, horse boxes, prize cattle and ordinary livestock. To avoid congestion, in 1907 a 1,644 feet long Down goods loop opened followed in 1915 by an Up goods loop of 2,478 feet. Sidings for crippled wagons were laid in 1924, and additional sidings in the Up and Down yards were opened in October 1944 offering 13 roads in the south yard and 17 in the north. The Up goods loop became the Up reception siding on 23rd April, 1969; similarly the Down goods loop became the Down reception siding. During the Second World War Westbury was a base for ambulance trains.

In 1899 Westbury was provided with three signal boxes: North, Middle and South, placed respectively at the Up end of the passenger platform, at the Down end of the platform and at the junction of the Salisbury branch. The Middle box closed 5th May, 1968 (it was replaced by the reception sidings ground frame until closure 13th May, 1984), ; the South box closed on 16th September, 1978 and was replaced by a miniature panel in the North box which was renamed Westbury, the 99-lever mechanical frame

Staff on the steps of a signal box at Westbury probably in the 1920s.
Gerald Quartley collection

Hymek No. 7097 leaves Westbury 1st September, 1969 with the 17.23 Portsmouth Harbour–Cardiff., passing Westbury North box on its way.
Revd Alan Newman

being shortened by one lever. On 3nd June, 1979 the miniature panel was extended to include Warminster allowing the box there to be closed, Westbury itself eventually closing on 27th April, 1984. A new power box for the area came into use on 13th May, 1984, temporary signalling arrangements used during the intermediate fortnight.

On 11th June, 1927 the GWR opened a bus depot at Westbury, operating a service to Dilton Marsh via several routes. A Thornycroft 'A.1' bus was used initially, joined later by a 32-seat Maudslay as passenger traffic increased. It is believed that during the summer of 1928 a Sunday service ran between Bratton, Westbury and Dilton Marsh and certainly with the introduction of the winter timetable on 24th September, 1928, a Sunday service was operated between Trowbridge, Westbury, Dilton Marsh and Frome. With the summer timetable commencing 8th July, 1929, it was joined by a service from Bratton to Frome. From 29th September, 1928 on Wednesdays, market day at Frome, the Westbury and Dilton Marsh service was extended to that town. By agreement with the Western National dated 30th August, 1929, the GWR bus services from Westbury, together with the vehicles, passed into Western National hands the following day, though the GWR acted as an agent for the Western National and continued to operate those services until 26th March, 1929.

To the north of Westbury station were the ironworks of the Westbury Iron Co Ltd served by its own siding from broad gauge days. When the

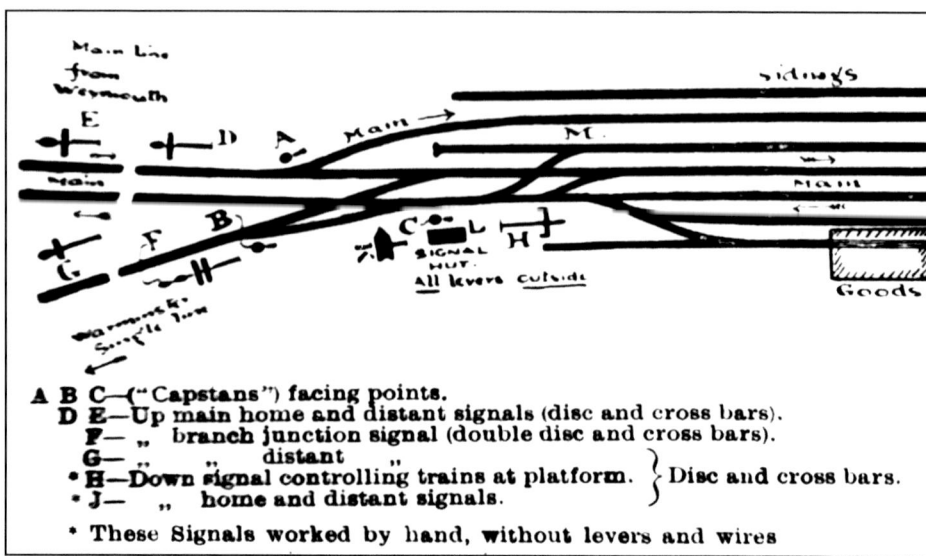

Diagram of Westbury circa 1900.

WSWR was being built it was discovered that the navvies were cutting through iron ore. On 24th July, 1857 a dozen men formed a company to excavate and smelt the ore, one of these men being Rowland Brotherhood who held the contract for building the Salisbury branch. Some shareholders also held interests in collieries accessed from the Frome to Radstock mineral branch. A ton of ore needed a ton of coal to make 8 hundredweight of pig iron. At the iron company's works, Brotherhood laid the sidings and manufactured the boiler, hoists, furnace bands and other fittings in addition to supplying £10,000 worth of ore and coal wagons. The ore had been first quarried in 1856, but the two blast furnaces did not begin operations until 1858. Partly due to very poor management the company went bankrupt in 1859, but the works was reopened in 1861 by the Wiltshire Iron Company, Brotherhood erecting a third furnace. The ore was extracted on the open-cast system.

In 1869 100,000 tons of ore were extracted, but over the years the industry fluctuated. The internal standard and narrow gauge lines had their own locomotives from the mid-1870s, two of each gauge, the 2 feet gauge system connecting the buildings and also the adjacent iron ore mines.

In the mid- 1880s one large furnace with a cubic capacity as large as two of the others was erected and only one was used subsequently. The product was confined to pig iron, the output sometimes amounting to 800 to 900 tons per fortnight.

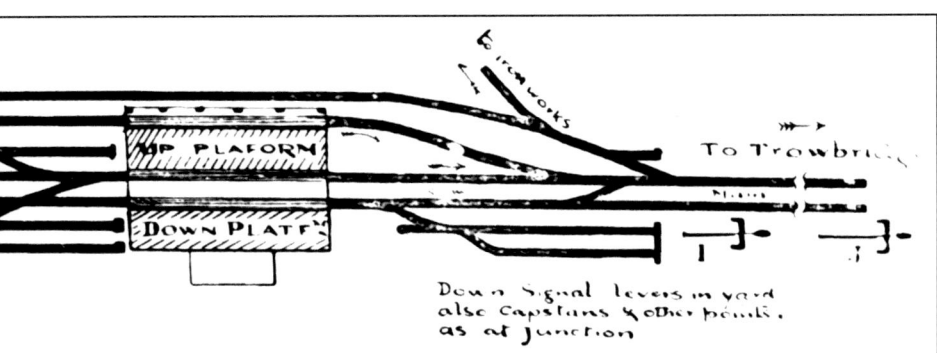

*K—Down caution signal for main line.
L—Signal hut.
M—Catch point.

A 28XX class 2-8-0 heads an empty passenger train past Westbury Iron Works in the late 1930s.
Brian Willson

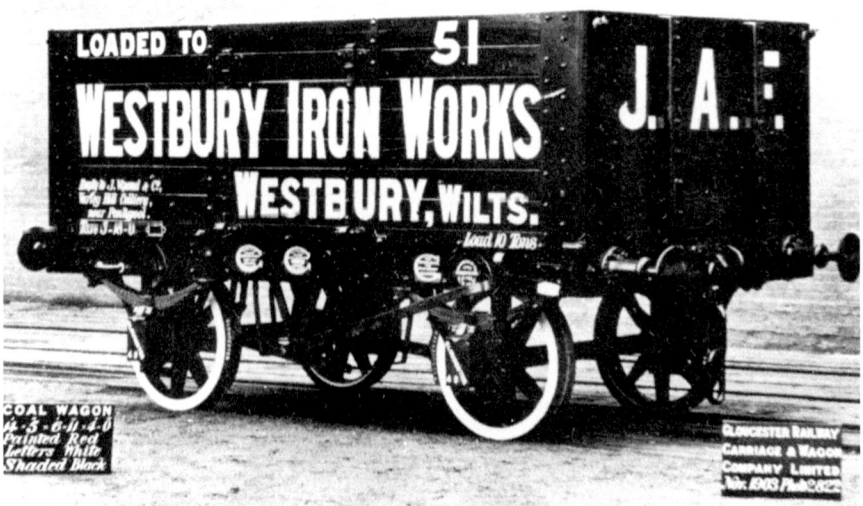

Red-liveried Westbury Iron Works wagon No. 51 built November 1903.
Author's collection

Few other ironworks in the land were so excellently situated being in the countryside with a good atmosphere and pleasant surroundings near the ore's source (so expense for the carriage of the raw material was low) and adjacent to a coalfield and a railway.

On 9th February, 1901 the following notice was posted at the works:

> Westbury Iron CompanyLimited
>
> All the workmen in the employ of this company take notice these works will close on Saturday, 23rd February instant, when all engagements with workmen will cease.
>
> By order of the directors,
> J. R. Tennear, Secretary

At the beginning of the week commencing 17th February the fires were withdrawn and the men occupied in clearing up, this keeping them busy until the time of the notice expired. The 200 men threatened with unemployment, knowing that other work in the neighbourhood would be impossible to find, attempted to avert their loss by offering to accept a reduction in wages equal to 10 per cent, the amount by which their wages had been raised previously. The directors were unable to reverse their decision but the blow fell less heavily on the surrounding villages than on Westbury itself as village homes possessed large gardens for growing vegetables.

The cause of the slump was obscure as six months previously trade was flourishing and management could not supply iron as fast as it was required and the workers enjoyed good wages. In shipyards ships had been lying in the stocks for months waiting for iron and all steel and ironworks were working night and day. Due to the high demand prices were so high that some orders were not made, a few shipbuilders waiting for prices to fall. Then inside three months 20 furnaces closed in the Cleveland district. The iron market must have been very speculative as Westbury held a large stock. Foreign competition, chiefly from the USA also had a hand in the matter as their up-to-date methods could put iron and steel more cheaply on the market.

Two meetings were held at Bristol on 18th February, 1901. The first was that of the directors of the iron company, followed by that of the shareholders at which this resolution was unanimously carried:

> That it has been proved to the satisfaction of the meeting that the company cannot, by reason of its liabilities, continue its business, and that it is advisable to wind up the same, and accordingly the company be wound up voluntarily.

The creditors held a meeting that afternoon and it was stated that if the business was wound up carefully, all creditors would practically be paid in full. The colliery and quarry owned by the company would be retained and with the help of shareholders and creditors combined, the works might be opened at an early date.

The Westbury Iron Company, with a capital of between £70,000 – £80,000 despite its advantages of nearness to ore, a railway and cheapness of labour, never enjoyed brilliant commercial success and even in brisk times of trade, only one 2½ per cent dividend had been declared since 1890. The decision to close was regrettable as there was still plenty of iron ore in the neighbourhood, but being financially weak the company could not just make iron and put it into stock for later sale. Closure to some extent affected the miners as 1,200 tons less coal was required each fortnight.

A new company reopened the concern in June 1903 running until the blast furnaces closed again in 1908, but iron ore extraction continued and as it was sold as a coal gas purifier until 1923. Thereafter most of the site remained disused until the plant and remaining locomotives were sold at auction in February 1939. Subsequently various civil engineering companies occupied the site; the former quarries are now lakes.

As part of the government scheme to relieve unemployment, a Westbury avoiding line was built to the south of the station complex and opened 1st January 1933. This avoided through-expresses having to slow to negotiate the curves at both ends of the station.

Almost immediately west of Westbury station, the Salisbury branch curved southwards away from the Weymouth line, was crossed by the Westbury avoiding line and climbed at 1 in 76/70 for approximately 2¼ miles. For a 28XX class 2-8-0 a maximum load of 30 loaded coal wagons was allowed up the bank to Upton Scudamore, but if banking assistance was sought, then the banker's allowance could be added. In the British Railways era, from 2nd April, 1950 the division between the Western and Southern Region was at milepost 111 between Westbury and Dilton Marsh, an appropriate board indicating the demarcation.

Dilton Marsh Halt (111 miles 11 chains – a mileage easy to remember) opened on 1st June, 1937. Each of the 300 feet long timber sleeper-built platforms was 8 feet wide, had a creosoted timber shelter and was electrically lit. Staggered, the Up platform is about 40 yards north of the Down. The estimated cost of the halt was £1,134. Its situation on a curve, combined with a steep gradient, sometimes caused starting problems for Down trains. The halt was unstaffed, but tickets could be purchased from an agent living at a nearby bungalow. Initially this was R. J. Mead,

56XX class 0-6-2T No. 6618, (88A Cardiff (East Dock) working through with the 2.35 am Radyr – Salisbury Yard East, climbs at 1 in 101 at the commencement of Upton Scudamore Bank 23nd April, 1955. It is about to cross the Westbury cut-off and on the right is the Down yard, the headshunt and the locomotive water tank. No. 6618 is assisted at the rear by its sister No. 5689. The bridge is shared with a public footpath from Dilton Marsh.

R. E. Toop

4-6-0 No. 5005 Manorbier Castle climbs the 1 in 75 through Dilton Marsh Halt with a Portsmouth train, 2nd July, 1955. Notice the sleeper-built platform. *R. E. Toop*

The Down platform of Dilton Marsh Halt with the Up platform beyond the far end of the Down, 27th April, 1963. *Author*

Dilton Marsh Up platform in metal 4th June, 1993. *Author*

Dilton Marsh Down platform 2nd June, 1994; the staggered Up platform can be seen below the 'Way Out' sign. *Author*

Information board re ticket purchase, 13th September, 1958. *Author*

cheap day returns being obtainable for such places as Westbury 3*d.*, Warminster 6*d.*, Bath 2*s.* 6*d.*, Bristol 3*s.* 9*d.*, Salisbury 3*s.* 0*d.* and Weymouth 7*s.* 9*d.* Approximately twelve trains called on weekdays in each direction and one each way on Sundays plus a late one to Warminster. Until 1969 tickets were purchased from the then local agent Mrs H. Roberts living in a nearby house. The suffix 'halt' was dropped from May 1969. Due to deterioration, about December 1969 both platforms were shortened to just one coach length.

It is certainly rare for a station platform to be stolen, but this is what happened on 30th September, 1988 when one of the aluminium platforms was pilfered. It was replaced with one of steel, but then the wooden sleepers holding back soil from the footpaths leading to the platforms were found to be rotten. The Health & Safety Executive declared that the new platforms were required to be at least as long as the longest train likely to call which was 58 metres. The villagers had been quite happy with the existing length of 15 metres and believed the extra expense was extravagant for the 20 or so passengers who used the station daily; sense prevailed and the Transport Secretary agreed with the villagers. For safety reasons the station was closed from 5th March to 30th April, 1994 for rebuilding in metal and concrete at a cost of £180,000. The work was made possible by funding from West Wiltshire District Council, Wiltshire County Council, British Rail and a £500 contribution from Dilton Marsh Parish Council. It was re-opened by Candida Lycett Green, daughter of Sir John Betjeman and displayed his poem *Dilton March Halt*.

> Was it worth keeping the Halt open
> We thought as we looked at the sky
> Red through the spread of the cedar tree
> With the evening train gone by?

O housewife safe in the comprehensive churning
Of the Warminster launderette!
O husband down at the depot with car in car-park!
The halt is waiting yet.

And when all the horrible roads are finally done for
And there's no petrol left to burn
Here to the Halt from Salisbury and Bristol
Steam trains will return.

Every year from 1994 about 100 to 120 villagers celebrated the re-opening of the halt by making a trip to Weymouth, Wales & West offering a special cheap rate on a through train; the railway company later made it difficult to set up and the trip ended about 2007. In the 2022 timetable 13 Up and nine Down trains are scheduled to call at Dilton Marsh on weekdays if requested, while on Sundays the numbers are nine and seven respectively. The station is used by approximately 20 passengers daily.

In 1941-1942 there were many servicemen using the trains so to offer more room for the military, one girl travelled from Dilton Marsh to Trowbridge High School only on Tuesdays, Wednesdays and Thursdays when she was given sufficient homework to cover her absence on Monday and Friday.

Beyond Dilton Marsh as the banker of a goods train approached the summit at Upton Scudamore, its driver would slightly close the regulator and the guard hearing this, would slowly apply his brake to ensure that all the couplings were taut in order to prevent one snapping when the train engine took all the weight.

At the summit was Upton Scudamore signal box (112 miles 69 chains) opened 10th December, 1900 together with a siding and crossover to avoid a banker having to work through to Warminster. In addition to breaking up the section between Westbury and Warminster, it allowed uncoupled banking engines to drop off here and return to Westbury, whereas if they continued to Warminster they needed to be coupled to the train to avoid being possibly separated on the ensuing descent. Passenger trains could be banked in the rear, uncoupled from Westbury to Upton Scudamore, but if it was to call at Dilton Marsh the banker was required to be coupled in front of the train engine. Because banking became less common, the signal box at Upton Scudamore was closed 20th August, 1964.

Upton had three signals on the Down road: Distant – which was rarely showed Caution as the Home and Starter signals were usually off to avoid the difficulty of starting a train on the gradient. A small refuge

DESCRIPTION OF THE LINE 49

43XX class 2-6-0 No. 6374 ascending towards Warminster banked by 56XX class 0-6-2T No. 5689, 12th May, 1956. Notice the two goats on the far side of the wire fence, they often appear in images at this location. The wagon behind the two bolgie bolsters is an ex-Ministry of Transport steel coal wagon, whereas at this date the majority of coal wagons were of timber.
R. E. Toop

53XX class 2-6-0 No. 6352 heads a train to Portsmouth banked in the rear by No. 5689, 16 July 1955. The first coaches are ex-LNER stock. *R. E. Toop*

siding on the Down side was provided for the banker if no immediate return path was available. While waiting, if it was autumn the fireman took the opportunity of mushrooming in nearby fields, the signalman from his higher vantage point directing him to the most fruitful areas. In exchange for this helpful advice, he expected his share of the pickings – no mushrooms, no more advice!

A well at Upton Scudamore provided water for the railway's use at Westbury, a 75,000 gallon tank on the Up side of the line at Upton supplying water by gravity. This tank was fed by a pump driven by either gas or electricity. A nearby pump house contained a 21 hp National gas engine running at 250 revolutions per minute, or a 25 hp electric motor at 248 revolutions per minute. The electric pump was controlled by Noflote control gear in the Upton tank and a low level float gear in the well. The gas engine was controlled manually.

On 6th September, 1922 an investigation was made into disused level crossings. Gates were at 112 miles 70 chains, 113 miles 13 chains and 113 miles 18½ chains. The gates at the three crossings were locked on 4th November, 1922 and as the permanent way inspector received no complaints, the gates at the last two crossings were removed on 3nd August, 1923 and the one situated near Upton Scudamore signal box removed in October/November 1923, the fences being made good. There were no roadways, these crossings being simply for accommodation purposes and had not been used for three years prior to October 1922. Similarly gates at 114 miles 10 chains and 130 miles 5 chains were removed about the same period.

Warminster (114 miles 36 chains) originally had a timber train shed similar to that at Westbury and Frome. When opened on 9th September, 1851 it was temporarily a terminus until the line was extended to Salisbury on 30th June, 1856. At this time there was a siding on the Up side at each end of the station together with a siding on the Down side where a short train could cross if it backed into the latter. The station was designed by J. H. Bertram, one of Brunel's chief assistants. The principal buildings are on the Up platform, passengers on the Down side provided with a timber waiting room originally heated by an open fire its chimney protruding behind galvanised-iron rear walls. As the original platform was a foot too low, it and the station buildings were raised by jacks to the standard height. On Easter Monday 1901 500 bookings were made from Warminster: 77 to Westbury; 40 to Salisbury; 32 to Bristol; 42 to Heytesbury; 26 to Frome and 273 to other destinations.

In 1903-4 the station was further improved at a cost of £4,000. This involved the platforms being lengthened to avoid expresses having to

Warminster 1878.

Warminster *circa* 1905: with milk churns on the platform. *Author's collection*

Warminster from the east, 27th April, 1963. *Author*

draw up twice; the waiting rooms were refurbished and a new parcels office, cloakroom and lavatories provided. A landing place was provided for milk to avoid hindering ordinary traffic. Goods siding capacity was doubled. On 19th June, 1904 the North and South signal boxes were closed and replaced by one box at the Down end of the Up platform. At some period J. Wallace Titt, a local manufacturer, erected a wind-powered pump on a free 12-months lease. At an unknown date, a lattice-style roofed footbridge linked the two platforms, but for economy its roof was removed in the latter part of the twentieth century.

In 1934 the train shed was removed and the platforms given individual canopies. A railway lorry service, cheaper than the local carter, was established at Warminster in 1928. Being so close to the Salisbury Plain army camps meant that the station was particularly busy during the Second World War with the movements of personnel and equipment, eight sidings, two loops and tank loading platforms being added. It had a timber-built goods shed with a central platform: railway wagons one side and road vehicles on the other..

At various times, various sidings served a creamery, Warminster Urban District Council Depot, the Air Ministry, (1942-1949), a banana warehouse and cattle pens. The station which was able to offer a full range of facilities, had a 12-ton crane and closed to goods traffic 2nd April, 1973. The gas works closed in 1947, gas then being piped from Bath.

When a banking engine worked through to Warminster, in order to avoid stopping to uncouple, unofficially the guard would lean out, lift the brake van coupling off the engine's hook, show the banker a white light to indicate that he had uncoupled before waving a white light to the train's driver to show that the banker had been uncoupled.

One night a banked train consisting of 20 fitted wagons at the front followed by 36 loose-coupled wagons, was worked by a Southern Region crew. Approaching Warminster at 35-40 mph, the driver of 0-6-2T No. 5689 banking realised that the SR driver had completely forgotten that he was coupled at the rear so to remind him to stop, applied the banker's brakes. The SR driver felt the tug and applied the brakes on his engine and the 20 fitted wagons. The 36 loose-coupled wagons, a foot between each, caught up and smashed into the first 20. The stop was so sudden that the fire-irons stored on the banker's tank top shot forward smashing the brake van windows and cutting the guard. The impact threw the fire of No. 5689 to the front of the firebox and caused the brick arch to come down on top of the fire.

The furious banking engine driver sprinted beside the 56 wagons and punched the SR driver on the nose. The Warminster signalman reacted

GREAT WESTERN RAILWAY.

WEST WILTS GOLF CLUB,
WARMINSTER.

Opening of the New Course

On Wednesday, April 3rd, 1907,

BY THE

Rt. Hon. A. J. Balfour, M.P.,

Who will join in

A FOURSOME at 11.15 a.m.,

With G. H. AITKEN, Esq. (the Captain) and the Professionals,

J. BRAID & H. VARDON
(Champion)   (Ex-Champion)

1.15.—Luncheon.   The Most Hon. the Marquis of Bath will preside.
2.45.—Exhibition Game by the Professionals.

TICKETS.—Visitors (Non-Members), 2s. 6d.; Ditto, ditto, Including Lunch, 5s. Luncheon—Members and Non-Members, 3s. 6d.; to be obtained of the Secretaries not later than 12 o'clock on Saturday, 30th March. After that time Luncheon Tickets, 4s. 6d.

Tea will be provided in the Marquee at 8d. per head.

(Rev.) H. L. DIXON
F. J. N. GLASS } Joint Secretaries, Warminster.

CHEAP TICKETS

1st, 2nd, and 3rd class, at about a single fare and a quarter for the double journey, minimum fare 1/-, will be issued by any train before 12 noon, to Warminster from Swindon, Malmesbury, Calne, Chippenham, Corsham, Bristol, Bath, Yeovil, Wells, Salisbury, Hungerford, Devizes, and intermediate stations.

PASSENGERS MAY RETURN BY ANY TRAIN THE SAME DAY.

Children under 12 years of Age, Half-price.   NO LUGGAGE ALLOWED.

The Tickets are not transferable. Should an Excursion or Cheap Ticket be used for any other Station than those named upon it, or by any other Train than those specified above, it will be rendered void, and therefore the fare paid will be liable to forfeiture, and the full Ordinary Fare will become chargeable.

For information respecting Pleasure Party and Excursion arrangements, and Special Trips on the Great Western Railway, application should be made to Mr. C. KISLINGBURY, Divisional Superintendent, Temple Meads Station, Bristol; or at any of the Stations.

JAMES C. INGLIS, General Manager.

Printed at the "Journal" Office, Market-place, Warminster.

Poster advertising a cheap ticket offer for a new golf course at Warminster, 1907.
Author's collection

by calling the police and an ambulance. This resulted in one driver being placed in an ambulance and the other driver placed under arrest. Their trains were left with two firemen neither passed to drive.

No road vehicle was available to bring replacement drivers to Warminster and the fact that both the Southern and Western Regions were involved added to the complication. The answer was to issue a wrong line order and bring a WR driver from Westbury on a light engine to work the banker, while a train from Salisbury brought an SR driver to work the stranded train forward. It ended reasonably happily as the police did not charge the WR driver with assault, but he was given a warning by the railway and the SR driver who caused the problem was severely censured and lost a week's pay.

In the 1980s the Royal Electrical & Mechanical Engineers had a workshop complex served by standard gauge sidings on the east side of the passenger station. Shunted originally by BR engines, from August 1976 a Ministry of Defence diesel locomotive was used. At the end of March 1977 this was ex-LMS 0-4-0 diesel-mechanical No. 7050 supplied by Drewry Car Co Limited in 1934; it had been built at the Dick, Kerr Works of the English Electric Co Limited with whom Drewry was associated from 1930 until 1941. It was sold to the War Department in 1943. When withdrawn in 1979 it was moved from Warminster to the National Railway Museum at York pending the completion of the Museum of Army Transport at Beverley, its final destination. Apart from the conversion to diesel-hydraulic from steam of 0-6-0T No. 1831 it had been the first LMS diesel locomotive.

18th July, 1998 saw a rail freight revival in the Army sidings when the first train for seven years arrived, conveying army vehicles from Dereham. They were used in an exercise and returned to Dereham by rail on 23nd July. Today the sidings are used occasionally.

Until 1874 a special method of train announcement was devised by the station master. A red signal arm was suspended by the windscreen at each end of the platform, the platform terminating by the windscreen. When a train was signalled as having left Heytesbury, or Westbury, a cord manipulated from the booking office where the telegraph apparatus was situated, raised the arm at the relevant end to horizontal. On the train's arrival, the cord was released and the arm fell to the normal vertical position. As with ordinary signals of the period, the arm at the Down end was differentiated by having two short pieces fixed at right angles to its end.

On 27th April, 1939 a siding was opened to Beechgrove Ordnance Depot east of Warminster at 115 miles 6 chains, with a new and enlarged layout with a new 28-lever signal box at 115 miles 11 chains brought into use 11th April, 1944. On 13th December, 1949 the box was closed and replaced by a ground frame which in turn was removed 3nd June, 1979; the ground frame was opened by a key electrically released from Warminster box. Army tanks and lorries were carried on Lowmacs and as the former provided a particularly heavy load, if the train was going down Upton Scudamore Bank the vacuum brake pipes would be connected to give a controlled descent and avoid a runaway.

A notable departure from Warminster was in late 1954 when a two-coach Royal Train hauled by Battle of Britain class No. 34060 *25 Squadron* of Exmouth Junction transported the Duke of Edinburgh from the town. Salisbury had sent an equally immaculate No. 34054 *Lord Beaverbrook* as standby, so the station was blessed by two Bulleids.

In March 1989 the town's civic society cleared years of accumulated rubble from near the car park and planted 110 trees: Norway and field maple, hazel, silver birch, cherry and willow. Paintwork on the Victorian footbridge was restored to its former blue and gold colours.

A fatal accident a Warminster station on Christmas Eve 1900 reveals the practices of contemporary passengers and facets of railway working.

Monsieur Alphonse Le Page, aged 54, living at Salisbury, taught languages at Warminster Grammar School and Emwell School. Arriving about 15 minutes before his train, the 5.30 pm from Bristol Stapleton

B963 Class 101 2-car set (W54191 driving trailer second), and W53613 (driving motor brake second) on crossover at Warminster being the 17.34 from Swindon changing to become the 18.40 to Swindon, 13th June, 1988. *Author*

Road forming the 6.55 Warminster–Salisbury, although both waiting rooms had fires, it was his custom to use the room on the Up platform as this was equipped with a table on which he could write. He remained there writing until his train arrived before crossing to the other platform.

Although a footbridge was provided, for speed he used the boarded luggage level crossing even after he had been warned on at least two occasions that this was a dangerous practice. On Christmas Eve he failed to notice an Up goods propelling five wagons, the first struck down the teacher, severing his right leg and injuring his left. As it is recorded that 13 wheels passed over Le Page, the shunting engine would have been a 0-6-0T, 2-4-0T or 0-4-2T. James Prosser, a relief signalman from Trowbridge, was walking beside the track to deliver a message when the light from his handlamp illuminated Le Page. Prosser immediately turned his handlamp red to prevent any further movement of the train and instructed Checker John Creed to tell driver Henry Tucker not to move his engine.

Station master Higgs applied a purpose-made tourniquet of India rubber to stop the bleeding before the patient was placed on a 4-wheel barrow and a Dr Willcox sent for. No time was wasted and Le Page arrived at the cottage hospital within about 20 minutes of the accident. Here Dr Willcox amputated both limbs; the patient recovered from the consequences of the anaesthetic, but 3 days later died from shock.

At the inquest Frank Davis, foreman porter said he had twice seen Le Page using the crossing and warned him of the danger and four notices informed passengers to cross by the bridge.

The coroner, F. T. Sylvester, unsympathetically remarked that Le Page could have used the waiting room on the Down Platform, but chose to use that on the Up, observing that 'Only venturesome, foolish persons would cross there, because there were so many lives lost each year on such crossings even by experienced persons'. He added that the railway company had erected a footbridge 'which was not only useful but ornamental, a quality which he was afraid they did not see very often in these bridges'. This surprising remark leads one to wonder if he was a GWR shareholder. Sylvester expressed gratification that the station master knew how to apply a tourniquet.

In 1934 a Warminster man, G. Morley Davies, set up what the *Great Western Railway Magazine* believed was a record for 'miles for money'. Mr Davies wrote:

> We were discussing in the train one morning the various facilities offered by the railway companies and the question of season ticket rates rose. I was

amazed to think of the value that a regular traveller gets from a season ticket, and my friend suggested that we ought to experiment with our tickets one day. I took his suggestion seriously, much to his surprise, and devoted a complete Saturday to determine how many miles of legitimate railway travel could, in one day, be squeezed out of my season ticket available between Warminster and Bristol. I left Warminster for Bristol and returned finally by the last train.

What I am desirous of knowing is, does it constitute any sort of a record for cheap travel? I have a feint idea that a Scotsman has me whacked! If so, I applaud his stoicism and bravery, as I was thoroughly 'fed up' at 10 p.m., after having travelled since 8.20 a.m.

Mr Davies calculates that, to the nearest half-mile, he covered 360½ railway miles. The cost for one day of his ticket, which is an ordinary third-class three monthly 'season,' works out at 1*s*. 8*d*., so that he travelled at the rate of 18 miles for a penny.

Many of the changes from train to train were made with somewhat narrow margins, but thanks to an excellent standard of time-keeping the "record"- if such it be – was not imperilled.

The following is the "log" of Mr Davies's journeyings:-

> Leaves Warminster 8.20: arrives Bristol 9.26
> Leaves Bristol 9.30: arrives Trowbridge 10.7
> Leaves Trowbridge 10.15: arrives Bristol 11.6
> Leaves Bristol 11.22: arrives Bradford 11.55
> Leaves Bradford 12.1: arrives Bristol 12.38
> Leaves Bristol 1.10: arrives Warminster 2.33
> Leaves Warminster 2.48: arrives Bristol 3.55
> Leaves Bristol 4.14: arrives Trowbridge 5.4
> Leaves Trowbridge 5.22: arrives Bath 5.49
> Leaves Bath 6.8: arrives Bradford 6.24
> Leaves Bradford 6.40: arrives Bath 7.1
> Leaves Bath 7.24: arrives Westbury 8.1
> Leaves Westbury 8.16: arrives Bath 8.50
> Leaves Bath 9.6: arrives Warminster 10.00

The line, gently undulating, generally falls between Warminster and Salisbury. The principal building at Heytesbury, (118 miles 18 chains), was on what became the Down platform when an Up platform with a small shelter and crossing loop opened 4th March, 1877. Like the other stations between Warminster and Salisbury, it was designed by R. P. Brerton, one of Brunel's assistants. Built of local stone, the offices were contained in an economical chalet-style building, with a short canopy and tall chimney. A footbridge was never provided. The goods shed was of timber and stone.

Passenger and freight services were withdrawn as from 19th September, 1955, the station being almost half a mile from the village,

Warship class diesel-hydraulic No. 814 *Dragon* east of Warminster on the 10.50 Merehead-Fordam, 16th July, 1970. *Revd. Alan Newman*

A 4-4-0 heads a 4-coach salmon and brown LSWR set at Heytesbury on a train to Salisbury. *Author's collection*

Heytesbury view Down circa 1955: a van is in the loading dock and a grounded van behind the nameboard. *Lens of Sutton*

No. 5904 Kelham Hall calls at Heytesbury with the penultimate Down train, the 4.32 pm Bristol (Temple Meads)–Portsmouth, 17th September, 1955. *Hugh Ballantyne*

suffered from road competition. The signal box opened 4th March, 1877, closed on 5th May, 1963. Between 1916 and 1926 a line from the west end of the station served Sutton Veny Camp. The Down refuge siding was taken out of use on 4th April, 1954, but its Up counterpart lasted until 17th December, 1961.

One and a half miles beyond Heytesbury, Upton Lovell siding and ground frame came into use on 11th November, 1914, and was removed by 1925. A private halt for workmen came into use in November 1915, misspelt 'Upton Lovel' in the working timetable and was closed by the end of the First World War.

Codford, (120 miles 48 chains), had its principal building of stone on what became the Down platform. An Up platform with brick shelter and passing loop were added on 5th February, 1897 when the Down platform was extended at the east end. The line was doubled to Heytesbury in 1899 and to Wylye 13th January, 1900. For workmen building nearby First World War Army camps an additional shelter, with a large upward sloping canopy, was placed on the Down platform. The platforms were linked by a covered footbridge. The signal box

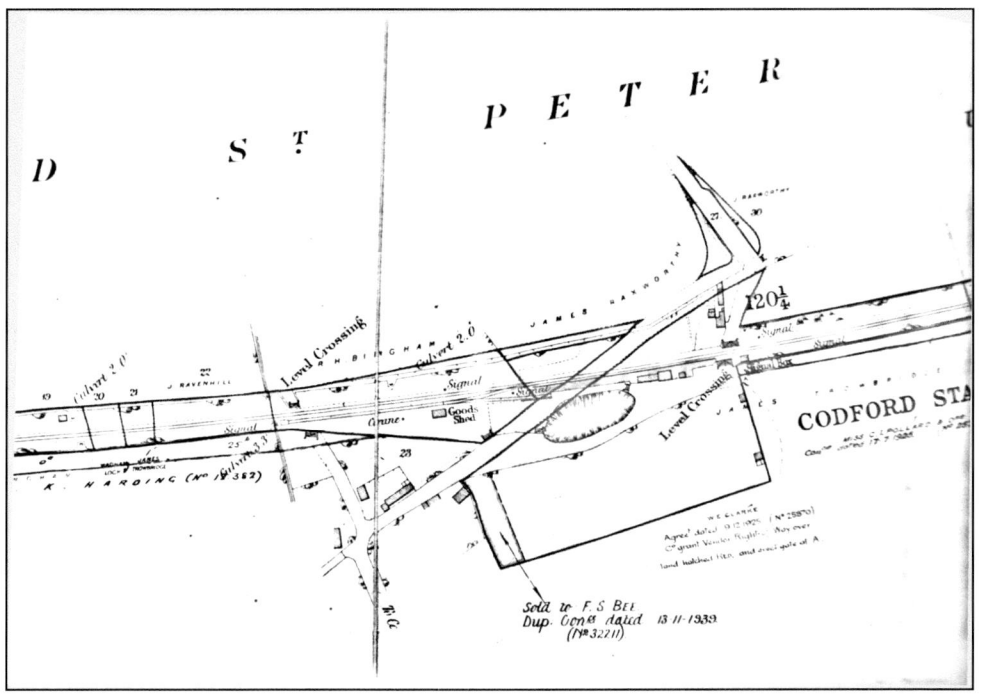

Codford 1878.

Codford view Down *circa* 1907. Signalman W. G. Pope at the foot of the steps; S and T plates hanging on front wall of signal box.
A. C. E. Notley

Codford view Down circa 1960: the additional shelter beyond the original office building which lacks a canopy. The timber goods shed is beyond the passenger station while the bracket signal by the goods shed offers access to the Down goods loop.
Lens of Sutton

DESCRIPTION OF THE LINE

Standard Goods 0-6-0 No. 514 at Codford *circa* 1910. No. 514 was withdrawn in August 1921.
Gerald Quartley

No. 5080 *Defiant* (86C Cardiff Canton) now preserved, pilots No. 4968 *Shotton Hall* with the last Up train to call at Codford the 5.02 pm Salisbury–Cardiff on 17th September, 1955. It stopped on time at 5.30 pm and nine passengers alighted. From October 1916 until January 1923 the siding in the foreground led to the military branch to Codford Camp.
Hugh Ballantyne

opened 5th March, 1877 was responsible for the level crossing. Initially gates provided protection but barriers came into use in 1976. The box closed in June 1982 with the instillation of automatic half-barriers.

A small timber goods shed was sited on the Down side at the Down end of the station, and the yard possessed a 3-ton crane, whereas most of the other stations only had a 30 hundredweight model. The station, which offered a full range of goods facilities, closed to this traffic on 10th June, 1963.

At the west end of the station the Codford Camp line opened in October 1914, closed on 1st January, 1923 and was lifted by 1924. In 1942 a 600 mm gauge railway was laid to serve Codford depot. At first wagons were propelled by hand, but from 1948 until its closure in 1960 four-wheeled diesel-mechanical locomotives were used, one built by Hunslet and the other two by Ruston Hornsby.

To cater for wartime traffic, goods loops were laid each side of the main line between Codford and Sherrington signal box (121 miles 3 chains); the Up loop came into use with the opening of Sherrington box on 30th December, 1914 and the Down loop opened 30th December, 1916. These were reduced to sidings 21st February, 1923 when the box closed, replaced by a ground frame to control the level crossing. Both loops were reinstated and a new 25-lever signal box opened on 27th May, 1943 and finally taken out of use 6th December, 1953 when Sherrington box was reduced to a ground frame before final closure 21st December, 1958 and the siding lifted April 1968. At 121 miles 27 chains was the 73-yard long Sherrington viaduct over the River Wylye. A platform at Stockton Crossing, about 1½ miles east of Codford, opened for use by workmen on some date after 1907, was in use in July 1915, but closed later that year.

Wylye (124 miles 34 chains) was Wiley until August 1874. The typical stone-built early GWR chalet-style building was on what became the Down platform; west of this structure was a cast-iron gentlemen's urinal. Originally a loading siding was provided on the Down side and a crossing siding on the Up. An Up platform and shelter were added in 1901 when the track was doubled and a large water tank stood at the west end of this platform. Water was pumped from a well by wind power. When the tank required replenishment, the vane was released so that it would turn the arms to the wind and water would be raised. The goods yard had a large timber-built shed, its large entrance betraying its broad gauge origins. West of the passenger station a Down refuge siding was laid about 1900 and extended in September 1908. Taken out of use in September 1968 it was reinstated 27th October, 1968. In 1943 three sidings were laid parallel with the Up refuge siding (laid *circa* 1901) to

A Down coal train trundles through Wylye. Wagons stand on the goods shed road.
Author's collection

A Barnum class 2-4-0 at Wylye.
Author's collection

serve the RAF Groveley Wood Depot until taken out of use about 1951. The addition of these sidings required a larger frame than could be fitted into the 1877 signal box, so this was replaced by a new box. The station closed to passengers 19th September, 1955 and to goods traffic, 2nd October, 1961; until then it had offered a full range of facilities. The signal box lasted until April 1982 when the 1973 level crossing barriers were automated.

The right bank of the River Wylye's flood-plain here for several miles is flanked by a river terrace and this site was used by the railway, but as it also provided the best site for settlements, where these occurred as at Stockton, Wylye, Hanging Langford, Little Langford and Great Wishford, the line passes above them crossing onto the chalk which formed solid rock on the valley sides. There is a dip between Wishford and Langford where 1 in 198 down becomes 1 in 198 up, this requiring the guard and enginemen to avoid snatching which could brake a coupling.

Langford station, (125 miles 12 chains) closed in October 1857. Wishford (129 miles 12 chains), originally with a single platform on the north side of the line, had an Up platform and crossing loop added in August 1896 causing the signal box to be relocated to the Down end of the Up platform. This box closed in 1901 when the track was doubled to

Wishford view Up showing the station master's house beyond the footbridge.

Author's collection

Wylye and Wilton and the replacement box set at the Down end of the Down platform. In July 1909 a covered footbridge was added. Also in 1909 a trailing siding off the Up line at the east end of the station was laid to a horse and cattle loading dock sufficiently long to take five wagons. It was built in order that A. P. Cuncliffe who owned extensive racing stables at Druid's Lodge could take his horses to racecourses. When J. V. Rank purchased the stables in 1934 he continued to use the facilities until about 1952. Soon after Rank took over the stables one of the horse box trains was hauled by an ex-Midland & South Western Junction Railway 2-4-0.

Wilton, (131 miles 53 chains), was given the suffix 'North' in September 1949 to distinguish it from Wilton South on the Southern Region's main line to the west. From opening it had two platforms, the principal building being on the Up side, but otherwise similar to the others on the branch which had theirs on the Down side. Down passengers were served by a small timber waiting shelter on the platform. A covered footbridge linked the platforms and unusually the roof remained in situ until the station's closure.

Wilton: Barnum class 2-4-0 No. 3208 heads a Cardiff–Portsmouth Harbour train composed of a 6-coach set of LSWR non-lavatory stock and a clerestory trailer, probably GWR. Most of the refuge siding on the right is bridge rail set on longitudinal sleepers. The fireman leans from the cab to see the guard's 'Right away'. *J. E. Kite*

Wilton North had a large goods shed and a 1½ ton crane; originally there was a loading siding on the Up side and a crossing siding on the Down. A Down refuge siding holding 39 wagons was brought into use on 18th June, 1901 and an Up refuge siding provided around the same date; latterly it was principally used for storing passenger rolling stock. The Wilton Carpet Factory provided goods traffic, while the gas works and workhouse both needed coal. Wilton Sheep Fairs were held in May and September, at one time some of the largest in the country when several thousand sheep changed hands each fair day, a significant proportion being despatched by rail. The station closed to goods 6th September, 1965; the signal box closed on 5th October, 1966 when all the sidings were taken out of use, though they were not lifted until 12th May, 1968. A sad ending in what had been Wiltshire's county town and indeed had put the 'Wilt' into Wiltshire.

One Sunday morning in the 1970s Wilton South signalman Barry Lake prevented a mishap. Greatly surprised when a gang of workmen arrived saying that they had come to demolish his signal box he advised that what they really had been sent to pull down was the ex-GWR Wilton North box which had been closed for several years.

With the transfer of the line to the Southern Region in 1950, matters had been rationalised by the Wilton South station master being additionally responsible for Wilton North, Wishford and Wylye.

In 2016 the local council produced plans for a Parkway station at Wilton on the site of the original station, the estimated cost for providing two platforms for 6-coach trains being £5.5m. It was thought that in addition to being served by Cardiff–Portsmouth trains, the Swindon–Westbury service might be extended; the estimated journey time Wilton–Salisbury was five minutes. Network Rail said that no money was available.

A quarter of a mile beyond Wilton North the LSWR from Exeter came alongside, and particularly in broad gauge days, was the scene of exciting races between the two companies. A physical junction here (132 miles 33 chains from Paddington and 85 miles 37 chains from Waterloo) was not made until 28th October, 1973 this allowing much of the remainder of the former GWR track between Wilton and Salisbury to be lifted. Wilton Junction was initially controlled from Wilton South signal box which had been renamed 'Wilton' on 28th October, 1973. The junction points were operated by point motors and all signals controlled by the box were colour lights. The Wilton signalman never actually saw his Salisbury to Westbury trains, just monitoring their progress on the track circuit diagram. Control of the junction was passed to the

DESCRIPTION OF THE LINE

Wilton 3nd May, 1934 the dock siding being used following the sheep fair.
Charles E. Brown

Interesting pointwork at the west end of Wilton North station. A wagon stands in the siding on the right. The Up road is of bull-head rail and the Down flat-bottomed.
Lens of Sutton

Ex-LMS Class 8F 2-8-0 No. 48431 passes Wilton North with a Down freight 8th April, 1964. As No. 48431 was allocated to Bath Green Park shed, an engine from the Somerset & Dorset line here would have been rare. *Author*

East of Wilton where the GWR and LSWR start to run alongside each other to Salisbury. A Class T9 4-4-0 heads the 3.00 pm Waterloo–Plymouth express. *Author's collection*

Salisbury panel when the box closed on 29th November, 1981; the panel was housed in the original 1859-1860 station building at Salisbury. As the timber and stone LSWR box at Wilton had become a rarity, it was dismantled and taken to the Mid-Hants Railway for preservation.

This junction was close to Tinkerpit Siding ground frame (132 miles 35 chains) the siding trailing in, opened 6th December, 1939 to serve two Anglo-American Oil Company sidings, both taken out of use 18th January, 1973. A short distance beyond, Quidhampton Siding ground frame (132 miles 54 chains) was brought into use 1st October, 1972 to serve English China Clays Calcium Carbonates Limited's quarry railhead, loaded trains of calcium carbonate slurry being sent to Inverurie, Aberdeenshire, for paper manufacture, initially via Speedlink but latterly by dedicated block trains. In 2023 there was talk of the sidings being re-opened to load containerised refuse for disposal. The erstwhile GWR line to Salisbury now terminates at a headshunt close to the 132¾ mile post. This is at the head of a 1 in 99 down incline where in unfitted brake days, goods trains stopped at a board to pin down brakes before descending. The fireman, with the aid of his coal pick, started pinning brakes, the driver moving the train forward until he estimated he had sufficient brake power to control the descent, when he

Robert Stephen Hawthorn diesel-hydraulic 0-4-0 Thomas shunter at the English China Clays Sidings, Quidhampton, 12th October, 1986. *Richard Giles*

would call his fireman back to the footplate. A goods train descended at 5-7 mph. Salisbury distant signal was permanently fixed at Caution and the Outer Home signal was on a track-circuit.

The GWR terminus at Salisbury, (134 miles 27 chains), lay alongside the site selected for the new London & South Western Railway station, though in fact the GWR terminus was built first. It was a typical Brunel train shed with two platforms and two central sidings. The Down platform had a smoke hood, but this was unnecessary for the other tracks as normally a locomotive would have stood outside. At right-angles to the buffers were the brick- and stone-built offices, now Grade II-listed. The canopy above entrance is decorated with lions' masks. The inside of the train shed roof was cantilevered from wooden cross-braced horizontal timbers with moulded brackets and square wooden posts. Outside the train shed both platforms had short umbrella-type canopies. In 1860 a covered footbridge offered access to the adjacent LSWR station which had opened in 1859. This bridge was only demolished in 1956 although the GWR terminus had closed to passenger traffic 12th September, 1932 when the two services still using it were diverted to the SR station. At least until 1925, one of the central carriage roads still consisted of longitudinal-sleepered track. This GWR terminus became a goods depot – though owing to a blockage at the SR Up platform, was at least once since closure pressed back into use as a passenger station. The Down platform and centre roads were taken out of use 5th November, 1967 and the Up 1st October, 1972, but it continued as a goods depot until early in 1991. Latterly the station was only able to offer facilities for general goods traffic and a dock for wheeled vehicles and livestock, but unable to cater for horse boxes, prize cattle, carriages and cars by passenger or parcels train. These facilities were all available at the adjacent ex-Southern Railway station.

As in passenger days the GWR station was 'open' a ticket platform was provided at the station throat, a short distance west of the Down platform.

Other nearby features were a two-road goods shed north of the passenger station and cattle pens near the station throat. A transhipment shed was placed between the GWR and LSWR, with a broad gauge and standard gauge track on either side of a central platform, a crane assisting transfer. The amount of traffic exchanged at Salisbury was relatively light as most of the GWR exchange traffic with the LSWR was carried out at Basingstoke. Until the change of gauge, employees of the two companies at Salisbury regarded one another with ill-concealed hostility. In August 1877, three years after gauge conversion, the two

Bulldog class 4-4-0 No. 3329 *Mars* at Salisbury circa 1929. A horse box and clerestory coach are on the right and the road between *Mars* and the coach is mainly on longitudinal sleepers. An extended canopy has been added to the arrival platform.

Author's collection

The interior of the GWR Salisbury station 1925. A smoke hood is provided above the arrival platform road, but unnecessary above the others as a locomotive would not have stood there for long. One road is on longitudinal sleepers. No run-round loop is provided. An arriving passenger train would either reverse out or have its engine released by a pilot engine.

GWR

PRIVATE AND NOT FOR PUBLICATION.

GREAT WESTERN AND LONDON & SOUTH WESTERN RAILWAYS.

AMENDED REGULATIONS

For Transfer of Passenger Trains and Loaded Vehicles with Passengers between the Great Western and London & South Western Lines at

SALISBURY.

To come into force on **MONDAY, June 16th, 1902.**

---

1. A Double Line Junction has now been laid between the G.W. and L. & S.W. Lines at Salisbury, one line leading from the G.W. Down Line to the L. & S.W. Up Platform, and the other Line leading from the L. & S.W. Down Platform to the G.W. Up Line. All Passenger Trains and Vehicles loaded with Passengers, including Horse Boxes with Grooms and Special Cattle Vehicles with Drovers in charge, must pass through this Direct Junction only.

2. Complete Through Trains must be worked under the following regulations:—

   (a) Trains from the Great Western Line to the London and South Western Line will be worked by the Great Western Engine to the South Western Up Platform, at which point the Great Western Engine will be released, and will return thence to the Great Western Yard. The Great Western Guard to give up possession of the train at the South Western Up Platform.

   (b) Trains from the South Western Line to the Great Western Line will be worked from the South Western Down Platform by a Great Western Engine. This Engine must be in prompt attendance, and stand ready to proceed to the South Western Down Station, under the direction of the S.W. Co.'s Shunter who must accompany the Engine until attached to its Train. The Train will be taken charge of by a Great Western Guard at the South Western Down Platform.

3. Through Vehicles loaded with Passengers, as shewn in Clause A, other than complete Trains, must in each case be pushed by the handing-over Company's Engine **in charge of a Foreman or Shunter**, but the Vehicles from the Great Western Line must be pushed over the Points clear of the locking bar opposite the R.C. House Number-taker's cabin, from which point the South Western Engine will take them forward. Vehicles from the South Western Line must not be pushed beyond the **Locking Bar** of the Points from whence the Great Western Engine will take them forward. Such Vehicles must be promptly removed from the Junction Line, but the handing-over Company's Foreman or Shunter must remain with the Vehicles until the other Company's man takes possession, and he will also be responsible for placing on the Vehicle or Vehicles at each end, after dark, a red lamp.

4. The G.W. Passenger Foreman, or during his absence the Goods Yard Foreman or Acting Foreman of the G.W. Co. or S.W. Co., as the case may be, must himself personally attend to the passing of all Vehicles with passengers in them to or from the South Western Line. The Station Master, Inspector or Foreman in charge is held responsible for personally supervising the work of Transfer of all Through Trains and Vehicles with Passengers in them, and for adopting every necessary precaution for safe working.

NOTE.—The speed of Trains running over the Junction Line, or during Shunting Operations, must not exceed 4 miles per hour.

These Instructions cancel those on pages 57 and 58 of No. 3 Appendix, dated January, 1901.

T. I. ALLEN,
Superintendent of Line.
H. HOLMES,
Superintendent of Line.

June 7th, 1902.

2,000. Arrowsmith, Printer, Quay Street, Bristol.

Amended regulations for transfer of passenger trains between the GWR and LSWR at Salisbury 7th June, 1902.

companies agreed to lay a connecting siding, each railway paying half of the estimated cost of £80. It was brought into use by February 1878, transfer of wagons being by either locomotives or horses; but as reversal was necessary it could not be used for through working. Cardiff-Portsmouth through trains started on 1st July, 1896 using a new direct connection brought into use just a few months previously; trains using it were restricted to a speed of 4 mph and the booked stop being at the LSWR station. A temporary double junction was brought into use in October 1899, but with the opening of the rebuilt LSWR station in 1901-2, the GWR laid a permanent double line junction to Platforms 1 and 3. Apart from regular use by trains to and from Southampton, it was useful for GWR through excursions to South Coast resorts and to military specials to the army bases being constructed on Salisbury Plain; at Salisbury the LSWR provided pilotmen and guards.

The original GWR signal box sited opposite the cattle pens closed on 27th May, 1900 when a replacement opened nearer the passenger station. The new box had a 95-lever frame reduced to 65 in 1972, was reduced to a ground frame on 27th October, 1973 and finally taken out of use 2nd December, 1973.

At Salisbury interchange operations were regulated by a ringing code between the GWR level crossing hut and the LSWR signal box. A double-arm LSWR signal was fixed at the transfer shed to regulate movements: one arm worked from the LSWR box and the other by the GWR crossing hut, the lever for the latter placed in the rear of the hut actually on LSWR territory.

The whole of the GWR yard from its western end at the level crossing, was only partly interlocked, so speed of all trains through the yard was restricted to 4 mph. Control of the yard was shared by two beats of bobbies who were responsible for signalling, locking of the scotch-blocks and also the point levers at various positions in the yard. These switchmen also collected passengers' tickets and the man at the eastern end of the yard assisted with platform duties. It was the custom to exhibit a white flag at the crossing for departing trains and green for arrivals.

Post-conversion the LSWR goods yard set east of its station on the Up side, was the exchange point for goods traffic between the GWR and LSWR. Carriage and wagon examiners checked loaded wagons and any unfit to travel were returned to the GWR by the GWR transfer engine. In the reverse direction, LSWR traffic to the GWR, mostly empty wagons, was worked by the LSWR to the GWR sidings west of the station and, following a carriage and wagon examination, any cripples were returned by the LSWR engine.

The Southern Railway regulations for 1934 stated:

Salisbury station. All trains, both Down and Up, must stop at this station.

Goods trains will be worked direct to the SR sidings at the Porton end of Salisbury station by GWR engines and staff.

On arrival of the train at the sidings, the Examiner must commence the examination of the wagons at once, and any wagons marked as unfit to travel to destination must be shunted out by the GWR engine and the SR staff; any wagons so marked must be taken by the GWR engine, van and Guard to the GWR yard, or worked to the 'cripples' siding in the west yard by SR engine and staff as arranged by the Examiner.

Trains will be worked to the GWR sidings by SR engines and staff. On reaching the GWR sidings the Examiner will commence the examination of wagons at once, and any wagons marked by him as unfit to travel to destination must be shunted out by the SR engine and GWR staff; any wagons so marked must be taken by the SR engine, van and Guard to the SR sidings for the necessary repairs to be carried out there.

Loaded wagons in coal trains arriving from the GWR which are carded for repairs but are fit to travel, and allowed to travel to their destination will, when returned in the empty coal trains to the GWR sidings, be shunted out by the GWR engines and staff, and dealt with by that Company.

Through trains from the GWR will be worked by that Company's engines and Guards to the SR Up local platform, and through trains from the SR to the GWR will be taken forward from the SR Down local platform by GWR engines and Guards.

Through vehicles, other than complete trains, must in each case be pushed into the Up local platform line in charge of a Shunter, who must remain with them until they are removed by an engine of the Company to which the transfer is made, and he will be responsible for placing a red lamp at each end of the vehicle during darkness, fog or falling snow.

The Inspector or Station Foreman on duty must personally supervise the transfer of all through trains and vehicles with passengers in them, and adopt any necessary precaution for safe working.

The heaviest transfer between the SR and GWR was in 1927 when an average of 780 wagons were exchanged daily. One point to be watched with trains from South Wales was that if destined for Portsmouth & Southsea (Low Level), as this station could only accommodate ten coaches, sometimes Salisbury was required to detach coaches from summer Saturday Western Region trains to Portsmouth to reduce them to this number.

The site of the former Great Western yard at Salisbury is now occupied by Salisbury Traincare Depot, opened on 1st July, 1993.

The first LSWR station at Salisbury was the terminus at Milford. It opened to passengers on 21st January, 1847; coal traffic started on 27th January followed by a Board of Trade Inspection on 23rd February and

DESCRIPTION OF THE LINE

The former GWR passenger terminus at Salisbury on 27th April, 1963 in use as a goods station following the removal of the train shed. *Author*

The exterior of the former GWR station at Salisbury 8th July, 1997. No. 37211 heads an Up train just visible on the left. *Author*

The former LSWR station still in use today on 8th July, 1997: the 1902 building is nearest with that of 1859 beyond. *Author*

A GWR 4-4-0 at the Salisbury SR station. *Author's collection*

W52094 Motor Second of a 4-car Inter-City set No. 1054 to Cardiff, 3nd July, 1966. The second car is W59821. Note the step to assist the porter taking shortcut across the tracks up to the platform. *J. Cull, Colin Roberts collection*

Diesel-hydraulic Type 4 No. 1019 *Western Challenger* at Salisbury 13th July, 1972 with empty stone wagons for Mendip quarries. *Revd. Alan Newman*

a full opening to all classes of traffic on 1st March, 1847. A service of five Down and four Up trains were operated on weekdays, but only one each way provided for all three classes, most trains being only first and second class. Two trains ran each way on Sundays. Before the arrival of the railway coal had cost 1s. 10d. a hundredweight; on the opening day it was 1s. 6d. and three days later 1s. 4d. The railway also brought salt for agriculturalists at a saving of 5s. 0d. a ton, the *Salisbury & Winchester Journal* observing that the use of more salt would benefit both salt and railway workers.

A shorter route from London via Andover was opened 1st May, 1857, but as a new through station just south of the GWR terminus was incomplete, initially trains via Andover set back into the existing Salisbury station at Milford. The extension of the LSWR to Gillingham on 2nd May, 1859 saw the new station opened adjacent to that of the GWR.

The two-storey building contained a booking office, booking hall, waiting room, refreshment room, offices and on the upper floor the station master's residence. Constructed in brick on a very restricted site, the adjacent GWR territory only allowed the LSWR sufficient space to build one platform. This was on the Down side, almost 800 feet in length and one of the longest platforms in England, and sheltered by a glass canopy covering both platform and the Down road. It could accommodate Up and Down trains simultaneously, but Up trains could not run in direct. They ran beyond the station to the ticket platform opened in 1862, making a prolonged stop until a vacancy arose at the main platform when they could then set back along the Down line into the station where the patient, or often infuriated, passengers were able to alight.

This arrangement was far from ideal and on 19th August, 1878 a narrow Up platform 683 feet in length was squeezed into the site partly using the position of the transfer shed, this being no longer required following gauge conversion and the installation of a physical link between the two companies. The Up platform could be accessed through a subway from the Down side. Buildings on the Up platform were of wooden, single-storey design containing booking office, waiting and refreshment rooms, toilets and offices; a short awning offered a certain degree of shelter. These temporary buildings were made to look more substantial by being painted and sanded to give an appearance of stone, nevertheless they served the city for almost 24 years.

Conditions at the LSWR Salisbury station were still far from ideal as more platforms were required and transfer between them made easier because the relationship between the GWR and LSWR had improved largely due to the development of through traffic. The solution was for the LSWR and GWR to exchange land, so this was done under an

Agreement of 28th January, 1898, including the relocation of the GWR engine shed for which the LSWR paid. A new double track connection was made between the two companies. On the Down side of the LSWR passenger station, adjacent to the 1859 building, a new two-storey establishment was executed by the main contractor J. T. Firbank in red brick relieved with Bath stone. It contained a spacious booking hall, booking and enquiry offices, refreshment and waiting rooms and a ramp to the subway linking the other platforms which also had waiting and refreshment rooms.

Two through platforms were provided in each direction. From north to south, Platform 1 was an Up through road; Platforms 2 and 3 on an island providing Down and Up roads respectively; Platform 4 was the Down road with Platform 5 forming a bay at its west end. Platform 6 was an Up bay. Platforms 1 to 4 were connected by a subway. The first of the new platforms came into use on 6th April, 1902 and the new double junction with the GWR on 7th June, 1902. The covered footbridge at the Up end, originally leading to the GWR station, was removed by the Southern Region in 1956. Platforms 1 and 3 were used by the GWR through trains, and following closure of the GWR station, also those terminating. Although Platforms 1 and 3 were joint in use and available to GWR staff, they were LSWR, not joint property. In spite of the fact that all four roads of the LSWR station were available to services between Waterloo and the West Country, only rarely did they use any but Platforms 2 and 4. Even on summer Saturdays the two platforms sufficed as they could take trains on the main line at a headway of nine minutes, even though every train had to be granted six minutes to take on water at Salisbury, except for the Atlantic Coast Express whose allowance was only five minutes.

The position of the GWR station meant that when the LSWR station was built it had to be located to the south of the GWR, thus introducing a 30 mph speed limit for the 8 chain curve at the east end of the station where an unobserved speed limit of 30 mph on 1st July, 1906 cost 28 people their lives. Thenceforth all passenger trains were required to stop at Salisbury, though in 1947 this order was relaxed for the non-stop 'Devon Belle' to pass through subject to a limit of 10 mph.

In 1986 British Railways was restructured so that what had been the Southern Region became Network Southeast, while the through trains from Cardiff and Bristol were operated by Regional Railways. With privatisation in 1995 the route from Waterloo was awarded to South West Trains while the Bristol to Portsmouth service was held by the Wales & West franchise operated by Prism, later replaced by Wessex. Freight services were run by English, Welsh & Scottish Railways and Freightliner.

35 exhibition vans on former GWR yard at Salisbury 5th October, 1986. *Richard Giles*

Salisbury view Down 24th May, 2018, 159106 on maintenance depot sidings set on the former GWR yard. *Author*

Chapter Five

Locomotives

Broad gauge engines appearing on the branch included the Leo class 2-4-0ST *Sagittarius* which headed the first train, fellow class member *Virgo*, Sun class 2-2-2ST *Javelin*, *Sun*, *Sunbeam*, Fire Fly class 2-2-2ST *Fire King*, Bogie class 4-4-0ST *Homer*, Premier class 0-6-0 *Bergion*, Ariadne class 0-6-0 *Nemesis* and Standard Goods 0-6-0 *Europa* and *Gladiator*. In 1873 *Europa* was shedded at Salisbury and except on Sundays, nightly worked to Bristol and back, its train known as the 'Bristol Goods' as far as Westbury, and then as the 'Salisbury Goods' onwards to Bristol. Hawthorn class 2-4-0s, particularly *Melling*, *Sharp* and *Stewart* were also used on the line as was Iron Duke class 4-2-2 *Lord of the Isles*. Hawthorn class 2-4-0s were used on stopping passenger trains and in 1877 some were rebuilt as saddle tanks. The Standard Goods *Europa* was the only one of its class to be rebuilt with a larger diameter boiler and to exist until the very end of the broad gauge being actually the last to leave Plymouth on 21st May, 1892.

These early engines certainly earned their keep. *Sun,* shedded at Bath worked the 7.30 am to Bristol before running to Chippenham and back, then headed the 1.30 pm Bristol to Salisbury and return reaching Bristol at 9.00 pm before the locomotive and coaches finally returned to Bath. There was only one driver and one fireman and both worked a long day.

0-6-0 *Europa*, originally built March 1853, here as rebuilt and the last broad gauge engine to leave Plymouth for Swindon 21st May, 1892. *Author's collection*

Hawthorn class 2-4-0 *Dewrance* built by Avonside Engine Company July 1865. It was not rebuilt and was withdrawn in May 1892. *Author's collection*

Broad gauge Hawthorn class 2-4-0ST *Stewart*, built by the Avonside Engine Company in January 1866 as a 2-4-0, altered to a saddle tank in 1877 and withdrawn May 1892.
Author's collection

Standard gauge Metro class 2-4-0T No. 632 which worked on the Salisbury branch. Built in 1871 with no cab, seen here as rebuilt in 1892 it was withdrawn November 1929.
Author's collection

Ex-Bristol & Exeter Railway standard gauge 2-4-0 No. 3 worked over the line as GWR No. 1335 and at one time the 481 class 2-4-0s, another Armstrong type, worked most passenger trains between Bristol and Salisbury but Armstrong's 717 class 2-4-0s also appeared. In 1880 William Dean's experimental locomotive No. 1 was tried between Bristol and Salisbury. Initially a 4-4-0T, in 1882 it became a 2-4-0T; free-running and popular, it lasted until 1924. It is recorded that in May 1898 a 2301 class 0-6-0 worked the 10.00 am Bristol to Salisbury which consisted of a brake third, a tri-composite, a composite, third and brake third. In 1906 a member of the same class worked the 9.15 am Weston-super-Mare to Salisbury.

517 class 0-4-2Ts working on the line included:

Date	517 class	Train
16.9.1897	1470	1.05 pm Salisbury–Bristol Temple Meads
22.1.1898	552	6.00 pm Bristol TM–Salisbury
5.7.1898	552	4.10 pm Portishead–Salisbury
29.7.1898	848	8.40 pm Bristol TM–Salisbury–Bristol

In January 1901 Duke class 4-4-0 No. 3316 *Guernsey* and No. 3317 *Jersey* were shedded at Salisbury, while the Duke allocation in January 1910 was just No. 3313 *Cotswold*.

Westbury, view Down *circa* 1905: a 517 class 0-4-2T stands at the platform with an Up train comprised mainly of 4-wheeled coaches. Westbury North signal box is on the right.

Author's collection

The spring of 1905 saw steam railmotors No. 3 and No. 5 sent to Trowbridge shed to work trips, including those to Warminster. In 1911 one Trowbridge car with trailer, worked to Salisbury on Sundays, returning on Monday morning. From October 1905 to November 1928 one of the Frome cars made a daily trip to Warminster.

Between 1912 and 1922 4-4-0s of the Badminton, Atbara and Flower classes worked passenger services between Cardiff and Salisbury.

In October 1913 a Mondays-only train was run from Bristol (Temple Meads) to Southampton and return, its GWR engine working through to Southampton despite the fact that locomotives were normally changed at Salisbury. Similarly 1914 saw Great Western excursions from Bristol to Bournemouth West and Portsmouth worked throughout by GWR engines, with the LSWR providing pilotmen and guards. Likewise engines on GWR military specials to the army camp at Bulford served by a branch from the LSWR's Salisbury to Andover main line, ran through, although the LSWR often supplied an assisting engine for the 1 in 55 bank between Newton Tony and Amesbury.

Engines of through trains were normally changed at Salisbury and of note is that GWR enginemen sometimes experienced a problem when taking over an SR train due to the GWR vacuum being 25 inches and that of the SR 21 inches. This meant that it was sometimes difficult to release the brakes because on the SR only the lower part of the brake cylinders became smooth and shiny, leaving the upper part rusty and not allowing the pistons freedom. Sometimes a significant volume of steam was used attempting to get the brakes off. Illustrating the problem is that in 1947 an average of 16 minutes was allowed for an SR/GWR engine change, compared with just five minutes for changing locomotives on a Waterloo to Exeter express.

The problem was avoided on certain trains when from about 1930 one Southern engine each day worked through to Bristol and back. T9 class 4-4-0s Nos. 713, 727 and 729 were noted and also from the early 1930s a D15 4-4-0 from Salisbury shed worked every evening to Bristol and back. Later in the thirties the author as a young child can remember seeing U class 2-6-0s, the now preserved No. 1635 being one of those used, on the 4.20 pm from Salisbury–Bristol but was fast asleep when it returned on the 9.00 pm Mail.

In the mid-thirties a highlight of the week for railway enthusiasts was a milk train which left Codford for London mid-afternoon with a passenger brake hauled by an Old Oak Common shed Star class locomotive, followed shortly after by a 4-coach passenger train for Bristol headed by by a Castle which for some years was the only occasion one worked over the line.

In the 1930s 4-4-0s were still common on passenger workings, but 4-6-0s of the Saint, Star or Hall variety, or 2-6-0s were becoming a more frequent sight.

Streamlined diesel railcars Nos. 10, 11 and 12 with lavatory accommodation started work from Bristol to Weymouth and Salisbury on 16th March, 1936. An observer in September 1938 noted that passenger trains were worked by Bulldog class 4-4-0s and 4-6-0s of the Saint, Star, Castle, Manor, Grange and Hall classes.

During the Second World War the SR loaned S15 class 4-6-0 goods locomotives to the GWR and although generally diagrammed for freight working, Nos. 496 and 498 were often observed working passenger trains on the line. Placed in the same power group as a Hall class 4-6-0, they were inscribed 'D' on a red disc on the cab side. During and after the Second World War LMS Stanier 8F 2-8-0s and their War Department counterparts made appearances on the line. In the latter days of steam, banking from Westbury was generally performed by a 56XX class 0-6-2T. As the route colour was red, no Kings, Class 8 4-6-2, or 18000 gas turbine engines were seen. Although 2-8-0s of the 47XX class were barred from the Westbury to Salisbury line, No. 4701 did slip through during a locomotive shortage in the Second World War and No. 4707 of Southall reached Salisbury in 1958 and another appeared on a passenger working. In the fifties 4-6-2 Britannias were permitted but appearances were rare, principally a week's trial with No. 70027 *Rising Star* (86C,

SR N class 2-6-0 No. 1626 near Warminster with a Portsmouth–Bristol train, 18th June, 1936.
W. Vaughan-Jenkins

Badminton class 4-4-0 No. 4103 *Bessborough* at the Salisbury SR station 31st May, 1929. No. 4103 was withdrawn in April 1930.
H. C. Casserley

A Star class 4-6-0 at Warminster heads the 10.30 am Cardiff General–Portsmouth & Southsea circa 1947.
E. J. M. Hayward

Cardiff, Canton) on the 1.00 pm from Cardiff and the 5.20 pm return from Salisbury in July 1953.

In the early fifties the engine shunting Warminster goods yard daily was a Westbury Pannier tank, but one Saturday in 1953 this was replaced by veteran Dean Goods 0-6-0 No. 2340. As it had no work to do in the afternoon, the driver and fireman invited an eager group of spotters onto the footplate. A most enjoyable time was then spent on a classic GWR locomotive which was first withdrawn in June 1939 and then re-instated in February 1940 to help with the war effort; it survived at Westbury until June 1954. Another classic Salisbury line regular until her demise in October 1957 was the 1914-built Star 4-6-0 No. 4056 *Princess Margaret* and spotters recall that in 1957 she seemed to spend most of her time on Bristol to Salisbury trains. Late in 1953 an unlikely locomotive observed shunting at Warminster was No. 7405 of Oswestry and probably the only member of the class seen on the line, but similar 54XX class Pannier tanks from Westbury shed shared daily push-pull duties with 14XX 0-4-2Ts from Swindon until replaced by the first generation DMUs from 1957.

On 13th July, 1957 at Salisbury Pete Foreman witnessed a most unlikely locomotive change. A Portsmouth train arrived behind the first rebuilt light Pacific No. 34005 *Barnstaple* of Stewarts Lane running ex-works. This brand-new vision of British steam was inevitably replaced for the onward run by the very elderly No. 4056 *Princess Margaret*.

In 1956 G. Freeman Allen noted on passenger workings a BR Standard Class 4 4-6-0; Halls, Counties and Castles, while on freight work War Department and 28XX class 2-8-0s; 2-6-0s; 0-6-0s and eight-coupled tanks could be seen. In the Second World War ex-Rhymney Railway 0-6-2T No. 43 of Radyr once made its appearance on the line and in 1958 ex-works 0-6-2T No. 5605 of Merthyr arrived at Salisbury in lined-out Brunswick green livery. Manor class 4-6-0s were a rarity until August 1958 when No. 7805 *Broome Manor* was reallocated to Cardiff, Canton and appeared on through trains.

By 1959 Cardiff-based Britannias worked regularly to Salisbury No. 70022 *Tornado* and No. 70023 *Venus* frequently worked the line on passenger trains. On 27th June, 1959 Class 9 2-10-0 No. 92207 (82B) St. Philip's Marsh, worked Bristol–Salisbury with the 9.20 am Swansea–Brockenhurst and on 2nd July, 1959 No. 92003 drew a freight to Salisbury. The two Radyr 2-8-2Ts Nos. 7202/5 held the monopoly of the 2.35 am through freight from Radyr to Salisbury from 1950, except for occasional relief by No. 7242 of the same class, or more rarely a 56XX 0-6-2T. After arrival at Salisbury the engine returned light to Westbury

A variety at Westbury shed 29th March, 1965: BR Standard Class 5 4-6-0 No. 73018 (70G Weymouth), with brackets for Southern Region route discs on its smokebox door; diesel-hydraulic Hymek D7041 and 4-6-0 No. 6876 Kingsland Grange. *Revd Alan Newman*

to pick up a train of empties for Penarth North Curve. The heavy freight tanks were generally of the 72XX 2-8-2T series, the 42XX 2-8-0T class with their small bunkers being less suitable for a trip from South Wales, but No. 4267 of Newport, Ebbw Junction, was seen in 1958.

The gradual changeover to diesel traction occurred in April 1961 when the first Hymeks were shedded at Bristol, Bath Road and progressively replaced ex-GWR 4-6-0s on principal passenger trains. Noticeable in the subsequent two years was that surviving steam-hauled services were worked mainly by the more prestigious Castles and Counties in preference to the more mundane mixed-traffic Halls and Granges which had previously dominated the service. As the more powerful locomotives became redundant they were classed as 'UBA' - 'Use to Best Advantage' until they required shopping and then they were scrapped. By 1963 redundant Halls at Westbury shed had taken over Upton Scudamore banking duties from the 56XX 0-6-2Ts, but they, too, were soon replaced by Hymeks. As in steam days, the Hymeks only worked from Cardiff to Salisbury where they gave way to Southern steam for the remainder of the journey.

Southern locomotives such as light Pacifics, S15 and U classes from Salisbury shed were used right up to 1967 on trains originating at

Warminster for Southern Region destinations, these including chartered excursions and banana trains for Geest. 4th November, 1963 saw the visit of an N class 2-6-0 to Westbury; this was No. 31834 of Exmouth Junction. Probably the next to appear was No. 31870 at Warminster on 13th June, 1964 temporarily stopped at Warminster en route to the scrapyard together with two Q1 0-6-0s No. 33014 and No. 33029 which remained there for several weeks. Around this time a light Pacific worked a banana train through to Bristol Temple Meads.

A locomotive spotter who kept close observation of the line never saw any BR Standard class tank engines on the line, (except for those withdrawn and going to South Wales for breaking up), no Standard Class 2 2-6-0 and only one Class 4 which was Salisbury's No. 76005 heading a special Up train on 18 April 1957.

A most unlikely sighting was the appearance of a Jubilee class No. 45584 *North West Frontier* on 12th July, 1963. Since early 1962 Class 9F 2-10-0s from Saltley had worked oil trains throughout from Birmingham to Fawley, but on this occasion Saltley had substituted a Jubilee and surprised one spotter when he saw it pounding up Upton Scudamore Bank. Ex-LNER *Mallard* appeared on 16th March, 1963 en route from Southampton to Swindon.

In 1964 the Hymeks and coaches were replaced by the new Class 123 InterCity DMUs, but by 1969 the Hymeks were back for a brief time until their mass withdrawal in 1971-72. In 1968 on Saturdays an SR Type 3 loco D65XX worked to Cardiff from Portsmouth.

Responsibility for providing locomotives and coaching stock was changed from the Western to the Southern Region which in 1973 provided 3-car non-gangway DEMU Class 205 Hampshire units. Knowledgeable passengers selected one of the second class compartments in the composite trailer, this having the only toilet accommodation, other passengers had to rely on there being enough time at Salisbury to offer a comfort stop. Following the introduction of a 2-hour regular interval service Portsmouth–Bristol in May 1973, the 3H units became overcrowded as a result of the growth of patronage. The revised service from 1st July, 1974 used 3H and Cross-Country units in 6-car formation. *Circa* September 1975 the Cross-Country units were taken from the 3H units. During late September 1976 many Eastleigh-based 3H DEMUs were out of service and Class 33 locos hauled rakes of 4-TC units on 3H diagrams. On 2nd September, 1975 No. 33118 was in charge of 4-TC units No. 416 and No. 423.

With the introduction of the 1977-78 winter timetable, Bristol Bath Road shed used its recently-acquired Class 31/4s and through services

Brighton to Cardiff were restored. The summer timetable for 1980 saw the responsibility for stock being returned to the Southern which provided Class 33s from Eastleigh. The normal coach formation was five Mark 1s, but towards the end of locomotive working, trains frequently ran with only four coaches, or even three, causing overcrowding. The Class 33/1s with buck-eye couplings were unpopular at Cardiff and only rarely appeared on that leg of the service.

The Class 155 Super Sprinters at a cost of £600,000 each, based at Cardiff, began regular working on 16th May, 1988. They were severely criticised by cyclists. Christopher Hunt, secretary of the Bristol-based Cyclebag stated:

> If I want to make a day trip to Bath from Bristol it will cost me £2.40 for myself and £3 for my bicycle which doesn't even occupy a seat. On top of this I would have to book a space for my bicycle, perhaps several hours in advance, and if I wanted to travel with two cycling companions, we would not be allowed to use the same train as there is only space for two bicycles on each Sprinter.

Hitherto cyclists had enjoyed free and unrestricted carriage of their machines in guards' vans. In 1989 trouble was experienced with the doors on the Class 155 Sprinters which tended to open when they should have remained closed. The defective trains were returned to the manufacturers, Leyland Bus, at Workington, for repair and replaced by Class 156 Sprinters intended for Scotland. This emergency lasted for several months and in mid-1989 both classes could be seen working trains over the line.

From 28th November, 1988 Class 127 diesel parcel units were introduced for Cardiff–Southampton parcel train workings, but performance was found unsatisfactory and reverted to Class 50 haulage from 23rd January, 1989.

A severe storm on 25th January, 1990 caused various sections of the line between Bath, Westbury and Salisbury to be blocked by falling debris and for a few hours trains were replaced by buses Bath to Salisbury.

From May 1990 the 08.35 Southampton–Temple Meads and the 11.48 return were worked by a 3H DEMU. Until then one had not be seen on the line for some time.

Express Sprinter Class 158 were phased in for Cardiff–Portsmouth from January 1991. They were capable of 90 mph, 15 mph faster than the earlier Sprinters and were equipped with full air-conditioning, wider seats, more leg-room and improved toilets, large enough to be entered by a wheel-chair. Some seats were separated by a table. Others faced the same direction with pull-down tables on the back of the seat in front.

LOCOMOTIVES

33019 enters Salisbury with the 06.30 Cardiff Central–Portsmouth Harbour, 21st June, 1986.
Author

2-car 158843 works the 06.35 Milford Haven–Portsmouth through Dilton Marsh on 2nd June 1994.
Author

Due to the seats being broader there were fewer than in the earlier Sprinters which had 79 or 84 seats whereas the Class 158s had 68 or 70. The last booked Class 155 was 155330 on 15th January, 1992.

From 28th November, 1992 Class 158 units were introduced on the Haverfordwest–Portsmouth Harbour and Portsmouth Harbour–Carmarthen services.

A feature of the summer timetable for 1993 was that it showed the 12.00 Saturdays- excepted Brighton to Cardiff not calling at Salisbury. This probably would have been the first regular passenger train not to call since the 'Devon Belle' stopped in 1954.

Until 2004 Wessex Trains between Cardiff and Portsmouth comprised only a 2-car set and at times theses were seriously overcrowded, but that year an additional car was added. From 29th May, 1994 one through train daily was provided from Cardiff via Westbury, Salisbury to Waterloo, the first worked by 158864. This offered useful access to the then-new Channel Tunnel Terminal at Waterloo or any other destination south of the Thames, but ceased running at the end of summer 1996 timetable as it was little used and on at least one occasion only carried four passengers. The first Carmarthen–Waterloo service on 30th May, 1994 was formed with 158867.

Arriva Trains Wales ceased to serve Waterloo after 22nd May, 2004 and only after considerable efforts by the West Wiltshire Rail Users' Group and others was the decision taken to transfer the Bristol to Waterloo services to South West Trains. Using one unit daily, it started and finished at Salisbury making two complete round trips. The service was again under threat in 2006 and apart from those living on the route who pressed for its retention, Bristolians feared the loss of a cheap day return to Waterloo for £25.10 compared with a First Great Western standard open return at £118 to Paddington.

From May 2017 Cardiff–Portsmouth services were predominantly operated by 5-car Turbo units.

Goods locomotives

In the 19th century three locomotives were required to overcome the maximum gradient of 1 in 70 ascending Upton Scudamore Bank and it was the practice that a heavy Down train could be divided at Westbury and worked in two halves up the bank, the engine returning from Warminster for the second half. For many years the mainstay for the long distance coal trains from Aberdare to Salisbury, 106 miles via the

Severn Tunnel, was the 1076 class or Buffalo 0-6-0ST, a Joseph Armstrong design. Coal trains of 36 10-ton wagons were worked from Bradford-on-Avon to Warminster up the bank by three saddle tank engines, but in the early twentieth century with the arrival of more powerful engines, coal trains were worked with one pilot.

The more powerful engines were the Aberdare class 2-6-0s which appeared in 1901. Based on the Atbara and Camel class 4-4-0s, many of the same parts were used but with 4-foot 7½-inch driving wheels. Three Atbaras were shedded at Salisbury in 1906 but were soon ousted when in October 1906 three 28XX class 2-8-0s were sent to Aberdare shed to work coal trains while three of the same class were shedded at Salisbury to return some of the empty wagons. An Aberdare class locomotive still retained one regular turn. In the Down direction a maximum of 55 mixed wagons was allowed to Warminster and 60 beyond.

An interesting turn was the 7.35 am Westbury–Salisbury pick-up goods, on Mondays worked by a 57XX class Pannier tank engine to change the Salisbury Yard Pilot, but during the rest of the week was a Swindon running-in turn which often occasioned a great deal of profanity from those drivers to whom they were given. En route to Salisbury the Westbury men changed over at Warminster or Heytesbury with Salisbury men working the 6.30 am Salisbury–Westbury goods, the regular locomotive being Bulldog class No. 3306 *Armorel*.

Bulldog class 4-4-0 No. 3335 *Tregothnan* at Westbury 27th May, 1935.

Colin Roberts collection

The 1930s saw the appearance on the line of the massive 72XX class 2-8-2Ts alongside the 28XX, 30XX 2-8-0s, 43XX 2-6-0s and 42XX 2-8-0Ts. The 42XX class 2-8-0s had been designed for short-distance coal traffic in South Wales, but following the General Strike of 1926 this traffic declined rendering some of the 2-8-0Ts superfluous. Collett realised that if the frames were extended by 4 feet 1 inch, the enlarged bunker could hold almost as much coal as a tender engine and thus allow the range of the class to be extended, some working to Salisbury. The enlarged bunker was supported by a trailing radial axle, creating a 2-8-2T of most impressive appearance entering traffic from the summer of 1934. Their coal supply of 6 tons and 2,500 gallons of water was not far short of the 28XX 2-8-0s tenders with 3,500 gallons and 7 tons respectively.

During the Second World War the following locomotives on loan to the GWR were allocated to Westbury: LMS Class 2F 0-6-0s : Nos. 3023 (10/39), 3048 (12/39), 3096 (1/40), 3517 (10/39), 3526 (12/39), 3543 (11/39), 3603 (12/39), 3689 (11/39); 3090 went later; only 3048 and 3096 stayed at Westbury throughout the war, the other engines being allocated to other GWR depots. All the LMS 2Fs were returned by November 1945. USA 160 class 2-8-0 Nos. 2422 (8/43) and 2434 (8/43) were later allocated to Swindon and all had left the GWR by November 1945. War Department 2-8-0 No. 7412 was allocated to Westbury from September-December 1944.

By the mid-1940s mineral trains were predominantly worked by eight-coupled tender or tank designs, though the 43XX class 2-6-0s were not infrequently seen.

Once during the Second World War a Rhymney Railway 0-6-2T worked a coal train from Aberdare to Salisbury. 56XX class 0-6-2Ts appeared on the line, particularly for banking, in the 1950s Nos. 5689, 6625 and 6699. They gave uncoupled rear-end assistance between 6.00 am and 10.00 pm, but during other times, as the Upton Scudamore box was switched out at night, a banker was required to be coupled at the rear and worked through to Warminster.

In *Careering With Steam* Arthur Turner relates that one morning when Upton Scudamore box was expected to be open, he banked a goods train up to that signal box and stopped letting the freight proceed. Arthur sounded the engine whistle, but to his surprise saw that the box was still closed, the signalman arriving late for duty. Arthur chased after the goods train and on arriving at Warminster sounded his whistle. The signalman there realised what had happened, let him into the platform and in due course returned to Westbury.

72XX class 2-8-2T No. 7205 with a Down goods, passes the closed Heytesbury station 27th March, 1963. *Author*

2884 class 2-8-0 No. 3850 takes a freight train from the WR to Salisbury goods yard, 18th October, 1962. *Revd. Alan Newman*

When an 0-6-2T was used for banking a passenger train to Warminster it was placed 'inside' the 4-6-0. This was because they were only fitted with a single-cone ejector, whereas the larger engines had four-cone ejectors which recreated vacuum faster after a brake application. Latterly bankers from Westbury to Upton Scudamore were mainly 43XX 2-6-0s. When a banker dropped off, the brake van's tail light was replaced in view of the signalman to indicate that the banker was leaving the train.

GWR-built LMS Class 8 2-8-0s worked some mineral trains on the line, for example on 31st August, 1945 LMS No. 8470 a Newport engine with a St. Philip's Marsh crew worked 44 empties on the 11.45 pm Salisbury to Aberdare; on 3rd January, 1946 No. 8464 a Cardiff Canton engine with a Salisbury crew worked 46 empties on the 11.25 am Salisbury to Aberdare; on 29th January, 1946 No. 8456 with a Westbury crew worked the 1.00 am Cardiff to Salisbury with 55 wagons and on 25th May, 1946 No. 8456 from Wrexham, Croes Newydd with a Newport crew worked the 6.50 pm with 42 wagons Aberdare to Salisbury.

Supplementary Operating Instructions issued September 1964 stated: 'To ensure the requisite brake power on falling gradients, all goods trains must have a proportion of train with operative automatic brake when load exceeds 22 basic wagon units, from Westbury–Salisbury, and 24 with diesel, and 35 with steam locomotives from Salisbury–Westbury.

Freight trains generally worked today by engines of Class 59, 66 or 70, a Class 59, are able to draw 2,200 tons up Upton Scudamore Bank unassisted.

At Warminster, 13th June, 1988, a Down stone train moves forward after banker 47079 has been uncoupled and seen here following the train to the crossover. *Author*

Locomotive Sheds
Westbury

A small locomotive shed opened in September 1848 but with the opening of a shed at Frome in 1854 its use declined and that at Westbury was closed about 1862. In February 1915 a new brick-built locomotive shed measuring 210 feet by 66 feet, with a slated roof, opened with four straight roads each capable of holding three tender engines or six tank engines, while a further road served the 84 feet by 40 feet repair shop equipped with lifting facilities. The nearby coal stage, 30 feet by 32 feet, was surmounted by a 45,000 gallon water tank. A 65-foot over-girder turntable was situated at the rear of the shed. Illumination for the shed and yard, originally by gas, was later replaced by electricity. During the Second World War brick and corrugated-iron shelters were built above the ash and coaling roads to conceal the glow of firebox clinker from enemy aircraft. On 31st December, 1947 the depot had an allocation of 71 locomotives. Originally with the GWR code WES, it was given the BR code 82D from 1949-1963 and 83C from 1963 until closure in September 1965. For the benefit of footplate crews who lived to the south of Westbury, a clinker path was laid beside the track from Dilton Marsh Halt to the depot.

A diesel depot on the site of the ambulance train sidings on the Up side of the line opened on 15th June, 1959 and lasted until 1st March,

The interior of Westbury shed 12th August, 1964: No. 4993 *Dalton Hall* nearest; No. 6874 *Haughton Grange* beyond. *Revd Alan Newman*

Westbury shed view east 1915: 2221 class (County Tank) 4-4-2T on the ash pit road and coal wagon No. 9071 inside the coaling stage. The sand drier house has a tall chimney.   *GWR*

The interior of the lifting shop at Westbury where the 50-ton power hoist is under construction, 1915.   *Author's collection*

Westbury line-up 21st May, 1965: 8750 class 0-6-0PT No. 3669 and No. 4673; 38XX 2-8-0 No. 3844 and ex-LMS Class 5 No. 44914. No. 44914 had been allocated to Bescot from new, so it was surprising to see it in this location. *Revd Alan Newman*

Class 4 d.e. No. 1668 at the new diesel shed, Westbury 26th July, 1973.
Revd. Alan Newman

The new GWR Salisbury shed in 1921. The sand furnace and chimney are to the right of the telegraph pole and the coal stage below the water tank. This shed closed in November 1950 when its engines were transferred to the Southern Region shed just visible on the opposite side of the line. *Author's collection*

Sand furnace and chimney at Salisbury in 1899. A 0-6-0 Dean Goods No. 2522 is on the left. *Author's collection*

1993. Since the 1970s locomotives allocated there were principally for working the heavy limestone traffic from the Mendip quarries at Whatley and Merehead.

Salisbury

The two-road broad gauge stone-built engine shed measuring 120 feet by 35 feet, with a gable and a slated roof, opened in April 1858, almost two years after the line reached Salisbury. It was set at the west end of the passenger station with a 45-foot diameter locomotive turntable nearby. Its first residents were *Javelin* and *Sunbeam* Sun class 2-2-2 saddle tanks. Following gauge conversion in 1874 all lines at Salisbury were standard gauge which meant that LSWR locomotives had access to the GWR turntable, though payment was required for its use. Certainly in 1882 Beattie's 348 class 4-4-0 No. 357 was noted as having used it, probably because the class was longer than any other on the line and the LSWR's 42-foot diameter table was too short.

In 1899 this shed was replaced by a new depot at the west end of the GWR's Salisbury complex, the LSWR bearing the cost as it required the land to expand its station. The three-road shed measuring 120 feet by 50 feet, was of brick, with a north light slated and glazed roof. The pits were unusually shallow. On the north side, en route to the turntable, was the coal stage, a water tank above holding 22,500 gallons. The depot, originally coded SAL, in 1932 became a sub-shed of Westbury, so its engines were labelled WES, but Salisbury still maintained a separate allocation. In BR days Westbury and Salisbury were coded 82D. An economy created by Nationalisation was the closure of former GWR shed on 26th November, 1950, Western Region engines from that date using the Southern depot, but the GWR 65-foot turntable was not removed until 17th August, 1958, as until that date it was useful to ease pressure on the Southern shed. An instance of this occurred in 1957 when the Southern Region's turntable at Salisbury was being replaced with one of 70 feet, a task taking several weeks.

The former GWR engine shed remained for many years storing preserved locomotives: Caledonian Railway 4-2-2 No. 123, the London & South Western Railway Adams 4-4-0 T3 class No. 453 and the London, Brighton & South Coast Railway 0-6-0T Terrier No. 82 *Boxhill*. The former GWR engine shed at Salisbury was eventually demolished to make way for the Salisbury Paper & Printing Depot of the British Transport Commission, officially opened 1st November, 1958.

Following closure of the former GWR shed, WR engines used the 10-road shed brick-built, with slated roof, (later replaced by asbestos), which had been opened by the LSWR in 1901. On its north side, forming the roof of what had been the enginemen's dormitory, was a vast water tank. Nearby was a 65-foot, (later replaced by a vacuum-operated one of 70-foot), diameter turntable and coaling stage. The depot, BR code 70E, closed in July 1967, but for almost a year after this date condemned locomotives were stored in the yard.

In 1956 Southern Salisbury men worked two daily turns to Bristol and back on Western engines; additionally Southern men also had a run through to Cardiff taking over the 9.33 am from Portsmouth & Southsea at Salisbury and returning on the 4.25 pm Cardiff–Portsmouth.

In 1956 G. Freeman Allen gathered that the Southern men took quite kindly to Castles and especially coveted their Automatic Train Control equipment, while Western men coming to Salisbury held the view that Swindon had nothing to touch a Bulleid Pacific in good fettle. On freight turns SR men worked no further than Westbury. At its peak, the Salisbury SR shed employed over 300 staff including 90 pairs of engine crews and 40 cleaners.

Much of the site of the former GWR goods yard was used for Network Southeast's DMU depot opened on 12th July, 1993. Apart from two sets, all the Class 159 units returned to the depot each night and as it was conveniently near the passenger station, fitters could be sent to any train needing immediate attention.

Warminster

From the opening of the line to Warminster on 9th September, 1851 until it was extended to Salisbury on 30th June, 1856, M Jolly in the Broad Gauge Society's Broadsheet No. 15 conjectures that Warminster had an engine house and certainly a turntable. Built of wood, the shed would have measured 21 feet by 85 feet. His conjecture is supported by a report in the *Salisbury & Winchester Journal* of 5th August, 1854 which records that a church service was held in the engine house at Warminster on 30th July, 1854.

Chapter Six

Timetables & Train Working

The opening timetable of the Warminster branch showed five trains each way daily and two on Sundays. Excursions were a good method of publicising the line and developing traffic. On 14th June, 1855 one ran from Warminster to Bristol, the *Salisbury & Winchester Journal* reporting 'Many of the inhabitants of the town, as well as towns between here and Corsham, embraced the opportunity of attending the Horticultural Show and the Zoological Gardens, Clifton, and enjoying a day's recreation for a very trifling disbursement'. As the direct line via Bradford-on-Avon had yet to be completed, the route would have been via Thingley Junction near Chippenham.

The first excursion train from Bristol to Salisbury ran on 14th August, 1856 and 'For the convenience of parties desirous of seeing the beautiful church at Wilton, the train will stop at that Station both going and returning.' A memorable excursion train ran to Salisbury on 22nd September, 1859, organised by the Wilts Friendly Society, a group which in pre-National Health Service days offered succour to members suffering illness. On 22nd September, 1859 members were invited to a grand festival at Salisbury, marching to the cathedral for a service in the morning and a dinner at the corn exchange in the evening. About 2,000 were expected from all parts of the county, though in the event, actually 2,600 members attended. The excursion from Devizes carried 101 in first class and 1,767 second class, a total of 1,868 in 33 coaches. As the train was too long to be handled at Salisbury station, it had to be split and was 'much delayed', so much so that instead of arriving at 10.15 am it did not arrive until almost 1.00 pm, its passengers missing the service at the cathedral. On the return journey some passengers had to be carried in goods wagons. The *Wilts Independent* had material for comment so its issue for 29th September, 1859 read:

> When things get to the worst there is some hope that they may mend; and, surely, so far as the traffic management of the Great Western Railway goes, the worst was arrived at on Thursday last, - this day week. Let us hope, then that amendment is at hand, for, most undoubtedly, it is sorely wanted. To have to go round miles and miles to the west, when your destination is eastward; to have to go, and to pay, for 110 miles in a journey hence to London, that same London being only 88 miles distant by the old coach road, is a sad nuisance; – and it is wrong as well, for the Directory have no right to charge their passengers for those weary miles of travel which they take because they choose to go a round-about way instead of a direct one. On no other line it is said, that such a wrong is perpetuated; the actual distance only, from place to place being charged. But

on this line it seems as if the Directors think the mere riding in their carriages a treat, and that it is that which ought to be paid for and not being conveyed to their destination. If they do think so they are very much mistaken, for the mere riding in a railway carriage, particularly second or third class, is no treat at all; the disagreeables are many, the comforts few. The chief advantage of railway travelling is speed: and if people are kept on the road, as hundreds and hundreds were last Thursday, a length of time sufficient to have walked the distance to Salisbury and back; the greatest of its advantages is lost. As Mr Fane truly and properly remarked, 'It is a scandal and a shame; and as a great commercial company I think they ought to return us all our money.' On the score of the delay alone, they ought to do this; but when it is considered that the delay was not the only loss, but that they did not reach Salisbury in time to take part in those proceedings which were the chief inducements to the journey, the return of the money is a simple act of justice. Well might Mr Fane call it 'A scandal and disgrace.' The delay on the road fully bore him out in so designating it. But how much greater the scandal and deeper the disgrace to have had no extra carriages to convey the people in except carriage trucks, – and of them not enough after having days, if not weeks, announced special trains for the purpose.

Were this a solitary instance it might be overlooked, but it is not so by many. Only a fortnight ago a party of excursionists who were delayed two hours on their down journey and who ought to have arrived here from Weymouth at half-past 8 o'clock in the evening, were kept on the road till two o'clock in the morning to their sore discomfort and to the terror of anxious friends and relatives who were expecting them. The question has been asked whether any one, or all of the persons thus delayed should not obtain redress through the County Court? It is said that they could and that each person might recover damages against the Company.

Down. Westbury to Salisbury.

Dist.	SINGLE LINE. STATIONS.	WEEK DAYS.								SUNDAYS.		
		1	2	3	4	5	6	7	8	1	2	3
		Goods	Pass.	Goods	Goods	Pass.	Pass.	Cattle	Pass.	Goods	Pass	
		a.m.	a.m.	a.m.	a.m.	p.m.	p.m.	p.m.	p.m.	a.m.	p.m.	
	Westbury dep.	6A 0	8 15	8 30	11•025	12 27	3 0	4 50	9 19	...	6 0	7 30
4¾	Warminster..dep.	6 30	8 27	10 0	12 0	12 40	3 12	5 10	8 25	...	6.30	7 45
8¼	Heytesbury	—	8 37	B	12 30	12 49	3 22	—	8 35	...	—	7 55
10¾	Codford	—	8 43	...	—	12 55	3 28	—	8 41	...	—	8 ▓
14¾	Wiley .. { arr. dep.	7 0 7•20	— 8 52	10 30 11 0	12 45 1•15	— 1• 4	• 3 37	5•30 5•40	• 8 50	...	7 0 7 10	— 8 ▓
19¼	Wishford	—	9 2	11 20	—	1 14	3 47	—	9 2	...	—	8 ▓
22	Wilton	7 45	9 10	11 45	2• 0	1 22	3 55	6 10	9 10	...	7.30	8 30
24¼	Salisbury..arr.	8 0	9 20	12 0	2 15	1 32	4 5	6 25	9 20	...	7 45	8 40

No. 1 A Does not run on Mondays.
No. 3 B to make two trips between Westbury and Warminster.
No. 7 Cattle Train will run only on Mondays, August 7th and 21st and every alternate Monday until further notice.

SALISBURY BRANCH.
Crossing of Trains.—Week Days.

The Up 6.40 a.m. Passenger from Salisbury, and the 6.0 a.m. Goods from Westbury, cross at Wiley
The Up 10.10 a.m. Passenger from Salisbury, and the 8.30 a.m. Goods from Westbury, cross at Wiley.
The Up 10.10 a.m. Passenger from Salisbury, and the 11.25 a.m. Goods from Westbury, cross at Westbury
The Up 1.40 p.m. Passenger from Salisbury, and the 11.25 a.m. Goods from Westbury, cross at Wilton.

This Line is worked by Single Needle Telegraph, under special instructions.

Timetable August 1871.

Following the change of gauge in 1874, the established service of five trains each way was increased to six with a fast Up train calling only at Warminster completing the journey in 43 minutes while the corresponding Down took 45 minutes; the other five trains each way were timed to take about 70 minutes. Only one train each way ran on Sundays.

In the early days timekeeping on the branch certainly left much to be desired, although the provision of a loop at Wilton in 1867 improved matters to some extent, meaning that the 10 miles to the first loop at Wiley was now punctuated by a loop just 2¾ miles from Salisbury, but matters were still far from ideal. For instance on 12th September, 1872 a train left Salisbury at 7.00 pm and only arrived at Bath at 11.00 having taken four hours for the journey of 41¼ miles. At Warminster it had been shunted into a siding and kept there for 1½ hours the only explanation given to passengers was that 'We must not proceed until we have orders from Westbury'.

The accident on 5th August, 1873 (see page 132) would have been avoided had the 1.30 pm from Bristol been on time – departure Bath at 1.57 pm and arrival Westbury 2.55 – but a regular user said in a letter to the *Bath Chronicle* of 7th August, 1873 that this train was usually late and recounted his experience when travelling from Bath to Warminster on 31st July, 1873.

I took my ticket in ample time and ascended to the platform, which was crowded to excess with passengers for the same train and the previous London

Salisbury to Westbury. *Up.*

SINGLE LINE.

Dist.	STATIONS		WEEK DAYS							SUNDAYS		
		1	2	3	4	5	6	7	8	1	2	3
			Pass.	Pass.	Pass.	Goods	Pass. & GOODS	Pass.	GOODS	Pass.		
			a.m.	a m.	p.m.	p.m.	p.m.	p.m.	p.m.	a.m.		
	Salisbury . dep.	...	6 40	10 10	1 40	2 30	4 45	6 40	7 30	8 5	...	...
2¼	Wilton { arr.	...	—	—	—	—	5 25	—	—	—	...	...
	{ dep.	...	6 48	10 18	1●48	2 45	5 5	6 48	7 55	8 12	...	...
5	Wishford	...	6 55	10 26	—	3 0	—	6 55	8 20	8 20	...	...
9¾	Wiley { arr.	...	—	—	—	3●25	5 25	—	8 40	—	...	...
	{ dep.	...	7● 5	10●36	2 2	3 40	5●35	7 5	9● 0	8 30	...	...
13¾	Codford	...	7 15	10 47	2 10	...	~	7 15	—	8 40	...	...
16	Heytesbury	...	7 22	10 55	2 17	...	5 55	7 22	C R	8 46	...	...
19¾	Warminster { arr.	...	7 30	11 4	2 25	4 10	6 15	7 30	9 30	8 55	...	...
	{ dep.	...	7 33	11 7	2 27	4 30	6 20	7 33	9 50	8 58	...	...
24¼	Westbury . arr.	...	7 43	11●20	2 37	4●50	6 40	7 45	10 5	9 10	...	...

SALISBURY BRANCH.
Crossing of Trains.—Week Days.

The Up 7.30 p.m. Goods from Salisbury, and the 2.0 p.m. Passenger from Westbury, cross at Wiley.
The Up 1.30 p.m. Goods from Salisbury, and the 4.50 p.m. Cattle Train from Westbury, cross at Westbury.
The Up 4.45 p.m. Goods from Salisbury, and the 4.50 p.m. Cattle Train from Westbury, cross at Wiley.
The Up 7.30 p.m. Goods from Salisbury, and the 8.13 p.m. Passenger from Westbury, cross at Wiley.
The 12.27 p.m. Passenger from Westbury passes the 11 25 a.m. Goods from Westbury at Wiley.

On Sundays, the Trains are so arranged as not to cross each other on the Single Line.

Timetable before gauge conversion. From *Salisbury & Winchester* Journal 2nd May, 1874

GREAT WESTERN RAILWAY.

SALISBURY TO MARLBOROUGH, BRISTOL, AND SWINDON.

Salisbury	6 30	*10 0	1 40	*4 35	6 50	Sun.—	8 5
Wilton	6 37	10 8	1 47	4 55	6 58		8 12
Wishford	6 44	10 16	1 54	...	7 6		8 20
Wiley	6 54	10 26	2 2	5 25	7 17		8 30
Codford	7 4	10 37	2 10	†	7 28		8 40
Heytesbury	7 10	10 45	2 17	5 45	7 35		8 46
Warminster	7 20	10 57	2 27	6 20	7 48		8 58
Westbury	7 30	11 10	2 37	6 40	7 58		9 15
Trowbridge	8 2	11 45	3 5	7 5	8 15		9 25
Devizes	8 14	12 50	3 40	...	8 45		...
Pewsey	8 37	1 35	4 7	...	...	‡ Stops at Codford on Tuesdays.	...
Marlborough	9 15	2 15	4 60	...	...		...
Chippenham	8 20	12 5	3 23	7 30	...		1 50
Swindon	8 55	12 50	4 0	8 7	...		3 25
Bradford	8 12	12 0	3 20	...	8 25		9 35
Bath	8 40	12 30	3 45	8 16	8 55		10 0
Bristol	9 20	1 0	4 25	8 55	9 30		10 35

SWINDON, BRISTOL, AND MARLBOROUGH TO SALISBURY.

Bristol	*6 25	10 20	*1 30	6 40		Sun.—	5 45
Bath	6 57	10 45	1 57	7 5			6 15
Bradford	7 27	11 17	2 30	7 35			6 45
Swindon	...	9 10	1 40	6 20			6 0
Chippenham	7 15	11 30	2 20	7 40			6 30
Marlborough	...	9 50	1 0	5 30			...
Pewsey	...	10 26	1 37	6 19			...
Devizes	7 5	10 55	2 5	7 0			...
Trowbridge	7 40	11 20	2 42	8 6			7 0
Westbury	8 15	12 17	3 10	8 25			7 30
Warminster	8 27	12 30	3 22	8 38			7 45
Heytesbury	8 37	12 40	3 32	8 48			7 55
Codford	8 43	12 46	3 38	8 54			8 1
Wiley	8 52	12 56	3 47	9 3			8 10
Wishford	9 2	1 7	3 57	9 15			8 22
Wilton	9 10	1 15	4 5	9 23			8 30
Salisbury	9 20	1 25	4 15	9 33			8 40

GREAT WESTERN RAILWAY.

BATH AND WEST OF ENGLAND AGRICULTURAL SHOW at BRISTOL, JUNE 8th to 12th inclusive

Ordinary Return Tickets to Bristol issued on SATURDAY, JUNE 6th, and following days, will be available up to SATURDAY, JUNE 13th, inclusive.

On THURSDAY and FRIDAY, JUNE 11th and 12th, an EXCURSION TRAIN for BRISTOL will leave Salisbury at 9.25; Wilton, 9.35; Wiley, 9.50; Codford, 10 0; Heytesbury, 10.5; Warminster, 10.15; Devizes, 9.50; Westbury, 10.30; Trowbridge, 10.50; and Bradford 11.10 a.m; and return from Bristol at 7.30 p.m. the same day. [5685

For fare and full particulars see Handbills.

Paddington Terminus, J. GRIERSON, General Manager.

Excursion 1874 advertised in the *Salisbury & Winchester Journal*, 6th June, 1874

GREAT WESTERN RAILWAY.

SALISBURY TO MARLBOROUGH, BRISTOL, AND SWINDON.

Salisbury	6 15	10 15	10 35	1 5	5 45	7 5	Sun.—	8 5
Wilton	6 24	...	10 44	1 14	5 54	7 14		8 12
Wishford	6 31	...	10 53	1 21	6 1	7 21		8 20
Wiley	6 43	...	11 5	1 32	6 13	7 32		8 30
Codford	6 52	...	11 14	1 40	6 22	7 41		8 40
Heytesbury	7 0	...	11 22	1 48	6 30	7 49		8 46
Warminster	7 13	10 48	11 42	2 5	6 43	8 2		8 58
Westbury {arr.	7 25	10 58	11 52	2 20	6 55	8 15		9 10
{dep.	7 35	11 10	12 10	2 30	7 10	8 20		1 0
Trowbridge	7 50	11 10	12 25	2 40	7 22	8 33		1 17
Devizes	8 12	...	1 0	3 45	7 45	...		5 50
Pewsey	8 37	...	1 30	4 15	8 15	...		6 20
Marlborough	9 5	...	2 5	4 50	8 25	...		...
Chippenham	8 20	...	12 56	3 7	7 52	...		1 50
Swindon	8 55	...	1 25	3 40	8 25	...		3 25
Bradford	8 15	11 20	12 52	3 15	7 50	8 45		9 35
Bath	8 45	11 40	1 25	3 50	8 25	9 17		10 0
Bristol	9 15	12 5	1 55	4 20	8 55	9 45		10 35

SWINDON, BRISTOL, AND MARLBOROUGH TO SALISBURY.

Bristol	6 20	10 25	11 50	2 10	5 20	6 45	Sun.—	5 45
Bath	6 50	10 50	12 15	2 30	5 53	7 13		6 14
Bradford	7 20	11 10	12 52	2 57	6 28	7 40		6 45
Swindon	...	9 0	12 25	2 10	...	7 20		6 0
Chippenham	7 10	10 15	12 55	2 50	...	7 48		6 30
Marlborough	...	9 30	12 5	...	...	5 50		...
Pewsey	...	9 40	12 37	...	...	6 19		...
Devizes	7 0	10 5	1 0	...	5 0	6 50		12 55
Trowbridge	7 45	11 20	1 27	3 22	6 40	8 15		7 0
Westbury {arr.	7 55	11 28	1 35	3 32	6 50	8 24		7 10
{dep	8 3	11 30	1 45	3 40	6 55	8 30		7 30
Warminster	8 15	11 42	2 5	3 53	7 7	8 43		7 45
Heytesbury	8 25	...	2 15	4 3	7 17	8 53		7 55
Codford	8 33	...	2 23	4 11	7 23	9 1		8 1
Wiley	8 44	...	2 34	4 22	7 32	9 12		8 10
Wishford	8 55	...	2 47	4 35	7 42	...		8 22
Wilton	9 2	...	2 54	4 42	7 50	9 30		8 30
Salisbury	9 10	12 15	3 0	4 50	8 0	9 40		8 40

GREAT WESTERN RAILWAY.

SUNDAY EXCURSIONS TO WEYMOUTH.

On SUNDAY, SEPTEMBER 1st, and *every* Sunday to end of OCTOBER, CHEAP EXCURSION TICKETS for WEYMOUTH will be issued from all Stations on SALISBURY BRANCH by Train leaving Salisbury at 6 20 a.m. Tickets available same day only.

For Fares see special Bills.

9359] J. GRIERSON, General Manager.

Excursions August 1878. From the *Salisbury & Winchester Journal* 31st August, 1878

Timetable after conversion. From *Salisbury & Winchester Journal* 11th July, 1874

train due at 1.35. But at 1.57 the London train had not arrived from Bristol and till that had passed there was no chance for me. At 2.12 came in the London Up train 37 minutes late. In seven minutes time that train was despatched, leaving the way clear for my Salisbury train. At 2.34 in came that train, also 37 minutes late. It took eight minutes to stow away the passengers and their luggage, but at 2.42, or just three-quarters of an hour after time we were despatched on our journey. We were due at Trowbridge 2.42, we reached it at 3.25 and were kept there nineteen minutes. We were due at Westbury 2.55, we reached it at 3.53. I was bound for the next station [Warminster] where we were due at 3.22, we reached it at 4.17, or fifty-five minutes after time. The length of the journey by road is seventeen miles [21½ by rail]. I have often walked it in 4¼ hours. By the aid of the Great Western I can do it in the greatly reduced time of 2 hours and twenty minutes. A rate of speed not actually less than eight miles an hour!!.

Just over two weeks after the change of gauge, a letter in the *Bath Chronicle* of 9th July, 1874 was critical of the timings on the branch and pointed out an anomaly:

The distance from Salisbury to Bristol is in the estimation of my worthy friend the traffic manager and his advisers is obviously more than the distance Bristol to Salisbury, or they would not have allowed on the average a quarter of an hour more for the journey than the other. The difference appears to be all the greater because, if I am not mistaken, the line where it departs from the strict level, slopes up to Salisbury and down from Salisbury, so that at first glance it would seem that the journey to Salisbury would take longer than the journey from that city. The train service generally, I am glad to observe, has been greatly improved – according to the new narrow gauge time table and will be of great advantage to the public – when it is worked according to the time table. At present the alteration is more one of fiction than fact.

When announcing the alteration of gauge the GWR officials claimed that greater punctuality and speed were to be the results, but this did not prove to be true. In the *Bath Chronicle* of 20th August, 1874 a letter written by F. S. said that his experience on 17th August

'convinced me that their "*improved service*" is a farce, and until they get some lessons or help from such lines as the Midland, London and North Western, or Great Northern, which is the best managed railway in the world, the Great Western will continue to be, as it ever has been, uncertain and inefficient. This morning, summoned to Southampton by the illness of a relative, I wanted as much time there as possible; accordingly I left by fast express train at 10.50 [a.m.] which runs in connection with the South Western train leaving Salisbury at 12.27 for Southampton. Although the train was a light one and without any extra traffic or luggage, we arrived too late for the South Western, which I afterwards ascertained had been kept waiting 5 minutes. Having to return to Bath the same day, my time in Southampton was limited to about an hour. On return the "improved service" was much the same. In the 7.05 [p.m.] train there were few passengers and little luggage, yet we were about an hour and a quarter getting over the first 11 miles beyond Salisbury [sic – Wiley station was actually 9¾ miles]. When we left Wylee [sic] it was 8.15 instead of 7.32 and we came into Bath late as usual.

A sarcastic letter appeared in the *Bath Chronicle* of 8th October, 1874.

> Travellers between Bath and Salisbury are under a great obligation to the Great Western Railway Company, not only for the arrangements which have been made for their comfort and convenience by the new time table, but for the marvellous fidelity with which those arrangements are carried out in practice.
>
> On 3 October I used the train which left Temple Meads at 1.50, Bath 2.10 and arrived Salisbury 4.50. For the last three months it has been timed to leave Bristol at 2.10 pm, leave Bath 2.30 and arrive Salisbury 4.50. A change in October added 20 minutes and the whole of this 20 minutes is spent at that delightful, airy and interesting spot, the Westbury station, or one of its sidings, whence the traveller is permitted to contemplate on the one hand, free of charge, the White Horse on Bratton Down, and, on the other, the slag and refuse of the Westbury Iron Works.
>
> After the customary struggle to get at the little hole in the booking office through which the tickets are issued – one of the charms of railway travelling in this country – I reached the platform. My train arrived at 2.27 and left at 2.30 – the old time. Scheduled to reach Westbury at 3.15, it arrived at 3.27. The London train was not in – it should have arrived at 3.32, but arrived 3.55 and left at 4.2. the Salisbury train should have started at 3.40, but left at 4.6; Warminster arrival should have been 3.53 but actually was 4.22.

A correspondent writing in the *Bath Chronicle* of 22nd October, 1874 said that on 10th October the 1.50 pm ex-Bristol Temple Meads was 17 minutes late at Bath, 12 minutes late at Westbury and 29 minutes at Warminster taking 2 hours 12 minutes to make a 17-mile journey. On Saturday 17th October he caught the 1.50 again. 'It was only 13 minutes late arriving at Bath and then was detained through some misfortune to the engine for eleven minutes and left Bath 24 minutes after time; was 14 minutes late at Westbury and 36 late at Warminster – 2 hours 19 minutes for 17 miles.

The story continued in the issue for 29th October, 1874. On 24th October the 1.50 was only one minute late arriving at Westbury. 'The truth, I have no doubt, was that the authorities at that station were quite unprepared for so unprecedented an event, and were thrown into some little confusion. The train had been only six minutes late leaving Bath, and the allowance of time for the journey to Westbury was so very liberal, that it had no difficulty in making up five of those six minutes and reaching Westbury one minute after time, or at 3.16 instead of 3.15.

But the force of nature – or at least GWR nature – could no further go. By a wise provision of the directors, the train to Salisbury is kept waiting at Westbury for 25 minutes, during which time it is arranged that the train from London to Weymouth shall arrive at, and be cleared from Westbury station. On Saturday it was 22 minutes late arriving at Westbury, cleared in 4½ minutes and the Salisbury passenger who ought to have left at 3.40, left at 4.4. Arrival at Warminster was 4.14, 21 minutes late instead of 3.53.'

The GWR authorities, feeling that action should be taken, in November amended the timetable so that the 1.50 from Bristol left at 2.10. On 7th November it left Bath punctually and arrived Westbury on time. Unfortunately the train from London was late as usual and arrived at six or seven minutes to four. This resulted in the Salisbury train arriving 16 minutes late at Warminster. On 14th November it was ten minutes late leaving Bath, 15 minutes late arriving at Westbury and the train from London was 37 minutes late.

Part of the trouble was caused at Westbury when four trains – from Paddington, Bristol, Weymouth and Salisbury were supposed to connect and since the alteration of gauge trains had been one and a half times the length and no train could discharge and reload passengers throughout its length without having to pull forward for the rear half to be at a platform.

The correspondent seemed to have solved the late train problem when on 28th November he caught a later train. This left Bristol at 5.20 pm, was on time 5.53 at Bath and arrived Warminster punctually at 7.7, there being no London train to wait for. Regarding the 2.10 he commented:

> It shows that western passengers who are most numerous are kept waiting unnecessarily at Westbury for the dilatory, if wise, men from the east.

Yet again, the *Bath Chronicle* revealed more criticism of the GWR in a letter of 5th April, 1877, its correspondent querying curious charges. A second class ticket from Bath to Southampton cost 9*s*. 8*d*., but on the journey in question, the writer was carrying 2 hundredweight of luggage – a hundredweight above the allowance for second class. He was charged an extra 7*s*. 0*d*., yet a third class ticket from Bath to Southampton was only 5*s*. 9*d*. so in effect he paid 3*d*. more for the carriage of a hundredweight of luggage than one would for a third class passenger.

The timetable for August 1887 offered six trains each way daily and one on Sundays. Most trains, which stopped at all stations, took about an hour between Westbury and Salisbury, though one omitting Wilton, Wishford, Codford and Heytesbury took 48 minutes.

In 1898 the 8.12 am Bristol to Salisbury was composed of a 6-wheel van; a first class coach, a second, three thirds and a 6-wheel van. The 8.40 pm Bristol to Salisbury was headed and tailed by a 6-wheel van and in between a bogie third, a bogie composite and a bogie third.

On 1st July, 1896 a through service from Cardiff to Portsmouth was inaugurated, two trains each way taking an average time of 4 hours 39 minutes for the 139.5 miles. They linked five ports: Cardiff, Newport, Bristol, Southampton and Portsmouth. As there were single line sections between Westbury and Salisbury until 1901, 3 mph slacks were imposed at crossing stations for the single line staff exchange to be carried out by hand. Demand for this through service was initially light and trains were required to call at many intermediate stations to justify their existence.

The Wilton to Salisbury section was doubled from 1st July, 1896 and with it a 'direct siding' opened to and from the LSWR at Salisbury. With this improved link came the inauguration of Cardiff to Portsmouth through passenger services on 1st July, 1896, but a note in a LSWR working timetable stated that through coaches were already running between Bristol and Portsmouth on one train each way, so it would seem that the 'direct siding' had come into use on a previous date, controlled at the GWR end from a ground frame and subject to a speed limit of 4 mph. Proving popular, the service was soon increased to four trains each way, these passing to and from the LSWR metals at Salisbury and using its station.

The January to April 1902 timetable showed ten trains each way daily between Westbury and Salisbury, two being Cardiff to Portsmouth and return. On Sundays there was only a local service, calling at all stations between Bristol and Salisbury, Up in the morning and Down in the evening.

The timetable for April 1910 showed twelve trains each way daily and two on Sundays. The 2.35 am Mondays excepted through from Portsmouth & Southsea to Cardiff, ran non-stop Salisbury to Warminster only setting down at Westbury for passengers from LSWR stations if they had informed the guard at Salisbury. It took 30 minutes to travel between Salisbury and Warminster. Mondays excepted, a 5.55 am one-class only steam railmotor calling at all stations ran from Salisbury to Westbury in 57 minutes. Other trains also took approximately an hour. Two through trains ran from Portsmouth & Southsea to Cardiff, one non-stop between Salisbury and Westbury, the other ran non-stop Salisbury to Warminster and did not call at Westbury. In total five through trains ran daily each way between Portsmouth and

WESTBURY and SALISBURY (1st and 3rd class).—Great Western.

Miles.	Down.	Week Days. mrn	mrn	mrn	mrn	mrn	aft	aft	aft	aft	aft	aft	aft	Sundays. aft	m
	62 Cardiff ....dep.	....	6 30	7 43	10i10	1120	....	12 5	3 15	4k25	....	5 30	7 15	1 25	3 42
	32 Bristol (Temple Mds) "	6 0	8g10	10 5	11c22	1h0	m	2 25	4c25	5c33	6 5	7 35	8 45	3 45	6 30
—	Westbury ....dep.	7 20	9 32	1122	12 24	2 18	3 6	3 43	5 26	6 36	7 30	9 3	9 38	5 16	7 58
4¾	Warminster	7 35	9 47	1135	12 38	2 32	3 17	3 57	5 40	6 50	7 44	9 18	9 50	5 30	8 12
8¼	Heytesbury	7 44	9 55	1143	....	2 39	Thurs. and Sats.	4 4	5 47	....	7 52	9 26	d	5 38	8 21
10¾	Codford	7 51	10 1	1149	....	2 45		4 10	5 53	....	7 58	9 32	d	5 44	8 27
14¼	Wylye	8 0	1010	1158	....	2 52		4 18	6 1	....	8 7	9 41	d	5 52	8 37
19¼	Wishford	8 10	1018	12 7	....	3 0		4 26	6 9	....	8 16	9 49	d	6 1	8 46
22	Wilton* ......[126, 140	8 18	1023	1214	....	3 6		4 33	6 16	....	8 23	9 56	d	6 8	8 52
24¼	Salisbury 120, 123, arr.	8 25	1035	1221	1 10	3 15		4 40	6 23	7 22	8 30	10 3	1025	6 15	9 0
49¾	140 Southampton † ....arr.	9‡46	1216	1 44	2‡21	4 27		....	7‡38	8‡10	1023	....	12 7	8 27	....
69¾	140 Portsmouth Town "	11 8	1240	2 25	3 48	4 50		....	8 16	9 17	1126	....	1247	8 40	....

Miles.	Up.	mrn		Week Days. mrn	mrn	mrn	mrn	mrn	mrn	aft	aft	aft	aft	aft	aft	Sundays. mrn	non
	142 Portsmouth Town dep.	1220		m	....	6 10	8n5	....	10 5	1220b	Thurs. & Sats.	2n5	....	5p0	5 56	1220	12 9
	142 Southampton † .... "	1 0		....	....	6 45	9‡15	‡	1123	1‡40		3‡15	....	6‡4	6 22	1 0	1242
—	Salisbury ....dep.	2 35	Mondays only.	5 55	7 45	9 15	10a10	1030	1 5	2a35		4a10	5 0	6a52	7 45	2 35	3 10
2¼	Wilton*	Except Mons.		6 2	7 53	9 23	....	1039	1 13	2 44		....	5 8	....	7 54	....	3 18
5¼	Wishford			6 8	7 59	9 29	....	1045	1 19	2 51		....	5 14	....	8 0	....	3 24
9¾	Wylye			6 18	8 9	9 39	....	1056	1 29	3 3		....	5 25	....	8 11	....	3 34
13½	Codford			6 27	8 17	9 48	....	11 5	1 37	3 12		....	5 34	....	8 19	....	3 43
16	Heytesbury			6 33	8 25	9 55	....	1112	1 41	3 20	m	....	5 41	....	8 27	....	3 50
19½	Warminster	3 5		6 43	8 35	10 7	....	1123	1 55	3 31	4 0	4 50	5 52	7 32	8 38	3 5	4 3
24¼	Westbury 32, 37 .....arr.	o		6 53	8 43	1017	10 50	1132	2 3	3 40	4 10	5 0	6 2	....	8 47	o	4 12
52¾	37 Bristol (Temple Mds) ar.	4 13		8 17	10 4	1139	11c50	1 41	3 33	4 57	....	6 10	7 27	8c43	1025	4 13	6 55
90½	58 Cardiff .... "	7 28		1014	1234	....	12 56	3 41	5 53	7 5	....	8 3	9 15	9 55	2 5	1046	8 13

a L. & S. W. Station.
b Through Train, Portsmouth to Bristol, see pages 142, 39, and 5.
c **Stapleton Road.**
d Stops to set down from Devizes, Melksham, and beyond, or Frome and beyond on informing Guard at Westbury.
g Through Train, Bristol to Portsmouth, see pages 13, 32, and 140.
h Through Train, Bristol to Portsmouth, see pages 15, 33, and 140.
i Through Train, Cardiff to Southampton and Portsmouth, see pages 62, 15, 33, and 140.
k Through Train, Cardiff to Southampton and Portsmouth, see pages 63, 17, 35, and 140.
m Motor Car, one class only.
n Through Train, Portsmouth and Southampton to Cardiff, see pages 142, 38, 3, and 59.
n Through Train, Portsmouth to Bristol, see pages 142, 39, and 5.
o Stops to set down from L. & S. W. Line on informing Guard at Salisbury.
p Through Train, Portsmouth and Southampton to Cardiff, see pages 142, 40, 7, and 60.
* Over ¼ mile to L. & S. W. Station.
† Town and Dock Station.
‡ **Southampton West.**

Passenger timetable April 1910

Oil-burning 4-6-0 No. 3950 *Garth Hall* on the 10.35 am Portsmouth–Cardiff 13th March, 1948. The upper part of the oil tank can be seen in the tender. *Pursey Short*

Cardiff. Thursdays and Saturdays one steam railmotor ran Westbury to Warminster and return. On Sundays two trains ran in each direction, one being a steam railmotor.

Following the reconstruction of the LSWR's Salisbury station, in October 1913 an extra train on Mondays-only ran from Bristol Temple Meads to Southampton and return, the GWR engine working through to Southampton.

In 1922 the Cardiff to Portsmouth was extended to carry through coaches to Brighton, though between November and April the service terminated at Salisbury. The timetable of July 1922 showed twelve trains each way daily Westbury–Salisbury, six of these being through trains,

Passenger timetable July 1922 Down.

TIMETABLES & TRAIN WORKING

one each way a luncheon and tea car train, and a motor train ran from Westbury to Warminster and return. The first Up train ran non-stop Salisbury to Trowbridge, though it called to set down at Westbury for passengers from LSWR stations who gave notice to the guard at Salisbury. The Sunday service offered one train from Bristol to Portsmouth and one Portsmouth to Bristol.

The timetable for July 1938 showed 14 trains daily in each direction: two through Cardiff to Portsmouth; two through Cardiff to Bournemouth West; one Cardiff to Brighton and one Bradford-on-Avon to Portsmouth & Southsea. Trains calling at all stations took about 50 minutes for the journey. On Sundays one ran through from Cardiff to

Passenger timetable July 1922 Up.

Streamlined rail car services circa 1937.

Portsmouth & Southsea, one Bristol to Portsmouth & Southsea and one Westbury to Warminster.

In the Up direction one Mondays-excepted ran non-stop Salisbury to Trowbridge though passengers from SR stations could ask the guard at Salisbury to have the train call at Westbury. Two trains ran Portsmouth & Southsea to Bristol, four Portsmouth & Southsea to Cardiff and two Brighton to Cardiff.

On Sundays four trains ran in the Up direction including one non-stop Salisbury to Trowbridge with an optional stop at Westbury and one Portsmouth & Southsea to Bristol.

With the war-timetable of September 1940 eight trains ran each way daily including one Down Bristol to Portsmouth & Southsea; one Cardiff to Portsmouth & Southsea and one Bristol to Southampton Terminus and one, except Saturdays, a school train from Trowbridge to Codford. Additionally four ran Westbury to Warminster and back. In the Up direction there was only one through train: that from Portsmouth & Southsea to Bristol.

August 1946 saw nine trains running each way on weekdays: four Bristol–Portsmouth & Southsea; one Bristol–Southampton Terminus; three Cardiff–Portsmouth & Southsea and one Cardiff–Brighton. There were five Portsmouth & Southsea–Bristol; three Portsmouth & Southsea–Cardiff and one Brighton–Cardiff; three trains each way ran Westbury to Warminster. The Sunday service was unbalanced: two Down and five Up. Due to the need for severe coal economy, in 1947 the service was reduced to five through trains daily Portsmouth to Bristol or Cardiff and four in the opposite direction.

In the 1950s timing of Salisbury to Westbury trains was over-generous, the 7.36 pm from Salisbury not being scheduled to leave Warminster until 8.10, thus allowing 34 minutes for the 20-mile run. Pete Foreman recalls a journey *circa* 1960 behind Bristol's excellent No. 6972 *Beningborough Hall* which made a mockery of this easy schedule. No. 6972 was in Warminster by 7.55 and its crew hurried over to Weeks' Cafe opposite the station for a quick refreshment before proceeding to Westbury on time, their progress on a par with the later Sprinters.

In August 1958 on weekdays 14 trains ran between Westbury and Salisbury, with as many as 28 on Saturdays, plus 16 goods trains on weekdays. An economy in train mileage occurred from 5th January, 1959 when the three trains between Portsmouth and Bristol reduced to just Salisbury–Bristol.

In 1962 the three daily trains between Cardiff and Brighton were supplemented between April and October by four between Bristol and

Diesel-electric multiple-unit No. 1106 passes Salisbury 'C' box working the 11.18 Bristol (Temple Meads)–Portsmouth, 8th October, 1973. *Revd. Alan Newman*

Brighton, while November to April the steam trains from Bristol terminated at Salisbury, diesel connections being made to Southampton and Portsmouth.

WR Inter-City DMUs took over service in June 1963, but 1965 saw the resumption of locomotive haulage with diesel-electric locomotives. May 1973 saw the introduction of a 2-hourly interval service introduced between Bristol and Portsmouth Harbour, while May 1979 saw the introduction of a Bristol Temple Meads to Brighton service.

From May 1988 the new 75 mph Class 155 Sprinters being introduced to replace Class 33 locomotives hauling Mark I stock saved nearly 20 minutes on a trip from Bristol to Portsmouth, also saving time on shorter journeys due to the Sprinters ability to accelerate quickly, a trip from Trowbridge to Bristol being about five minutes faster. Two trains daily ran from Bristol Temple Meads to Brighton instead of only one.

Before the end of the year the entire fleet of 35 Class 155 units had to be withdrawn following a passenger door opening while a set was moving. Some Class 156s formed temporary replacements until the problem could be resolved. When units from the Cardiff-based Class 155 were converted to the single car Class 153 they were replaced by Class 158.

By May 1992 the hourly Cardiff to Portsmouth express services called additionally at Trowbridge, the improved services to Southampton and

Weymouth creating 27 new jobs at the Westbury depot, many of the new staff being recruited locally. Over the previous 15 years the number of trains between Westbury and Salisbury had doubled to 21 each way. The summer timetable for 1993 showed a Brighton–Swansea train from 12th July–3nd September making a non-stop run Southampton to Bath; there was no corresponding return journey. The two Wales & West Railways Bristol–Waterloo (Carmarthen–Bristol–Waterloo) services which had been introduced proved so popular – they were particularly useful for Eurostar passengers as Waterloo was then the departure station for those using the Channel Tunnel – that from September 1997 an extra train was added to timetable. These three ran from Waterloo non-stop to Warminster, thence all stations to Bristol and Cardiff.

Wales & West's morning service to Waterloo 21st June – 3nd July, 1999 called additionally at Wimbledon for benefit of tennis fans and similarly called at Surbiton for gardeners wishing to attend Hampton Court Flower Show. In 2000 the Wales & West services came under the Wessex franchise.

In July and August 2002 Wessex Trains, in order to cope with the additional passengers using the Bristol–Weymouth service, hired from Fragonset Class 31s operated in multiple through the blue star wiring fitted to the Mk 2 coaches. Following a trial run on 8th September, 2002, the set began working the 12.00 Cardiff–Brighton and the 17.00 return just on Fridays, thus releasing a Class 156 for other duties on a busy day. In 2002 29 trains ran daily Westbury–Salisbury and in 2003, due to withdrawal of the Paddington–Fishguard boat train, the 19.17 Waterloo–Carmarthen was extended to Fishguard. In May 2003 the service was reduced to Bristol to Waterloo. Wessex Trains' use of locomotives ended late in 2005 and in April 2006 this train operating company was absorbed into the First Great Western franchise.

From 14th May, 2022 the GWR withdrew its services to Brighton. In 2024 27 trains ran each way between Westbury and Salisbury, most being through between Cardiff and Portsmouth Harbour, exceptions being a Swindon to Southampton Central, Swindon to Salisbury, two from Great Malvern to Salisbury, three South West trains from Yeovil Junction to Waterloo via Westbury and Salisbury, and three Filton Abbey Wood to Warminster. The Sunday service saw 17 Down trains, most from Cardiff, though one from Swindon to Salisbury.

There were 28 Up trains on weekdays, mostly Portsmouth Harbour to Cardiff, but one Fratton to Gloucester, one from Waterloo and one from Basingstoke. 15 passenger trains ran on Sundays.

Westbury–Salisbury is one of the few main lines which have never been used by a regular named train.

Freight

In the *Railway Magazine* for 1930 G. Grant, a retired GWR superintendent, wrote that the 7.00 am goods ex-Chippenham to Salisbury (probably *circa* 1870) was required to clear all traffic from Westbury for the branch, averaging three trips up Scudamore Bank and sometimes four. The head guard decided how many wagons the engine could manage and one head guard said that the margin between power and load was so slender at times that he and the underguard alighted and pushed to avoid dividing the train on the incline. The single line working could cause delay while waiting for an oncoming train and sometimes the 7.00 am goods reached Salisbury two hours late. As his guard's duty was booked for 12 hours, if the train was late it made a very long day.

Following gauge conversion, initially through coal traffic for Salisbury and beyond was attached to the two daily goods trains from Swindon, but June 1876 saw the Bullo Pit (Forest of Dean) to Westbury coal train extended through to Salisbury. Initially it travelled via Gloucester, the Severn Bridge not opening until 17th October, 1879. By 1884 it was joined by a through train from Aberdare, running as required.

Two developments had changed the whole aspect of the Salisbury branch – the opening of the Severn Tunnel in 1886 offered a shorter route from South Wales, coupled with the expanding demand for Welsh steam coal at Southampton and Portsmouth as sailing ships gave way to steamers. In 1888 only one through coal train ran daily but by 1893 this had increased to two regular and one conditional train daily to and from Aberdare, with another added in 1895. Although the locomotive and brake van ran through from Aberdare to Salisbury, in 1898 three of the five trains in each direction changed footplatemen and guards at Trowbridge, the other two changing at Newport. Salisbury and Trowbridge crews largely, but not entirely, worked trains between these stations, thus making a double journey a day's work, though it was not unknown for Trowbridge men to work to Aberdare and back. By 1907 a large Atlantic liner sailing from Southampton would burn up to 1,000 tons of coal every 24 hours which was two 50-wagon trains of coal daily. In 1917 283,353 tons of coal were carried to Southampton and 213,224 to Gosport. The 60-wagon coal trains worked onwards from Salisbury by Class 330 and 453 Drummond 4-6-0s. In 1909 coal trains from the GWR passing to the LSWR were: the 9.00 am to Portsmouth; 11.15 am locomotive coal to Basingstoke; 11.02 am to Bevois Park or Southampton; 2.23 pm to Bevois Park or Southampton; 4.30 pm to Bevois Park or Northam; 7.35 pm to Nine Elms. In the reverse direction empty wagon trains were worked by the LSWR to

Notice No. 234.   **PRIVATE AND NOT FOR PUBLICATION.**

GREAT WESTERN & SOUTH WESTERN RAILWAYS

Working Coal, Great Western to South Western,
AND
Empties, South Western to Great Western,
AT
SALISBURY.

TO COME INTO OPERATION ON MONDAY, APRIL 11th, 1904.

Trains of coal will be worked direct to the South Western Company's sidings at the east end of that Company's yard by the Great Western Company's engines and men, but each train will be piloted by a South Western pilotman, who will join the train at the Great Western signal box.

On the arrival of the train at the South Western sidings the South Western Company's examiners will commence the examination of the trucks at once, and any trucks marked off as unfit to travel to destination must be shunted out by the Great Western engine by the South Western staff, and any wagons so marked off must be taken by the Great Western engine, van and guard to the Great Western yard for the necessary repairs to be carried out there.

Trains of empties will be worked to the Great Western sidings by the South Western Company's engine and men. On reaching the latter point the Great Western Company's examiner will commence the examination of trucks at once, and any trucks marked off by him as unfit to travel to destination must be shunted out by the South Western engine by the Great Western staff, and any wagons so marked off must be taken by the South Western engine, van and guard to the South Western sidings for the necessary repairs to be carried out there.

Loaded trucks in coal trains arriving from the Great Western to the South Western sidings which are carded for repairs, but are fit to travel and are allowed to travel to their destination, will, when returned in the empty coal trains to the Great Western sidings, be shunted out by the Great Western Company's engines and staff and dealt with by that Company.

It is important that the Great Western engine and men be released as soon as possible after arrival at the South Western yard, and also the South Western engine and men after arrival at the Great Western yard, and return to their respective home depots.

(D. 23669.)

J. MORRIS, G.W.R.
H. HOLMES, L. & S.W.R.

April 6th, 1904.

(1500)   Arrowsmith, Printer, Quay Street, Bristol.   (D. 23669)

Regulations for transferring coal wagons
between the GWR and LSWR at Salisbury, 6th April, 1904.

the GWR sidings and, following carriage and wagon examination any cripples returned by the LSWR engine.

1927 was the heaviest year for wagon transfers at Salisbury an average of 780 wagons being exchanged daily.

In 1952 the branch pick-up goods left Westbury at 7.35 am, normally headed by a 28XX class 2-8-0, (or *circa* 1950 a 56XX class 0-6-2T often Nos. 5689, 6690 or 6699) and after shunting at the stations, was due into Salisbury shortly after noon; it left for Westbury at 6.00 pm where it was due at 9.10 pm. Due to traffic which accumulated over the week end, the Down Monday train was longer, sometimes requiring banking assistance to Upton Scudamore. There was also a local goods working that left Westbury at 2.15 pm, shunted the stations to Heytesbury and back before running light to Trowbridge where it became shunter there for the next 24 hours. The engine for this duty was usually a 57XX class 0-6-0PT or a 45XX 2-6-2T.

By 1954 on weekdays about a dozen goods trains ran over the line in each direction. One freight working in 1956 was the 10.00 pm Avonmouth–Salisbury; next day this locomotive worked the 3.07 pm (6.00 pm Saturdays only) Salisbury–Southampton Docks before working to Eastleigh on the 8.04 pm parcels from Southampton Docks (light engine on Saturdays). It then headed the 9.44 pm passenger from Eastleigh–Salisbury and finally the 3.30 am (Mondays excepted, and 4.30 am Sundays) freight from Salisbury–Avonmouth.

The announcement in September 1964 of the Bournemouth electrification meant that thousands of tons of ballast was required. Some came from the Southern Region's Meldon Quarry, but due to the long lengths of single line between Exeter and Salisbury, there were insufficient paths between passenger trains for this traffic, so for destinations east of Woking the stone trains were often routed between Exeter and Salisbury via Taunton and Westbury. Ballast was also supplied by Mendip quarries. This of course also travelled over the Westbury to Salisbury line.

In 2024 freight trains ran when required, usually six to ten on weekdays. Paths were allotted for: Merehead–Woking; Westbury–Fareham; Merehead–Woking; Merehead–Chichester; Merehead–Eastleigh; Quidhampton Sidings–Willesden Euroterminal; Whatley–Southampton.

In the Up direction were timetabled Southampton–Wentloog; Botley–Merehead; Eastleigh–Westbury; Bicester–Warminster; Kineton–Warminster; Crawley New Yard–Cardiff Docks; Fareham–Whatley; Ludgershall–Bicester; Marchwood–Kineton; Marchwood–Bicester; Ludgershall–Kineton; Chichester–Merehead and Woking–Merehead.

Chapter Seven

Signalling & Permanent Way

From its inauguration the line was equipped with the single needle electric telegraph to control crossing movements – initially the only crossing loop between Warminster and Salisbury was at Wiley. At first there were no signal cabins, points being interlocked with a signal by means of wire locking gear. Distant signals were worked independently and no starting signal was provided. Facing points were worked by an adjacent quadrant-type lever called a 'capstan', a coloured target affixed – red centre and white ring – indicating the position of the points. If set for the main line the target faced the train, but if for the siding it was turned edgeways. A quadrant had two pins for securing the points and a padlock for holding it in the normal position. The use of capstans continued until interlocking was introduced in 1876. The signals were the disc and crossbar type set on a rotatable post at right-angles so that only the disc or crossbar could be seen at a time. To avoid confusion, crossbar signals for the Up road were plain, whereas those for the Down road had portions pointing down. At night these signals displayed a red or white light. A signal post was often stayed with a guy wire. Until 1875 Westbury's signals were all disc and crossbar except for two 'fantails' removed before 1870. Disc and crossbars were moved by levers and points by capstan.

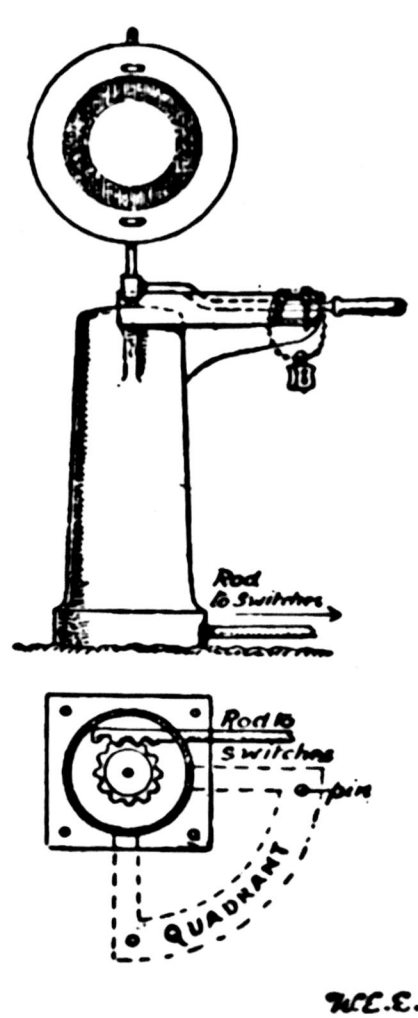

Combined signal and point lever.

Left: Wilts, Somerset & Weymouth Railway hand signals.

Below: Wilts, Somerset & Weymouth Railway fantail signals.

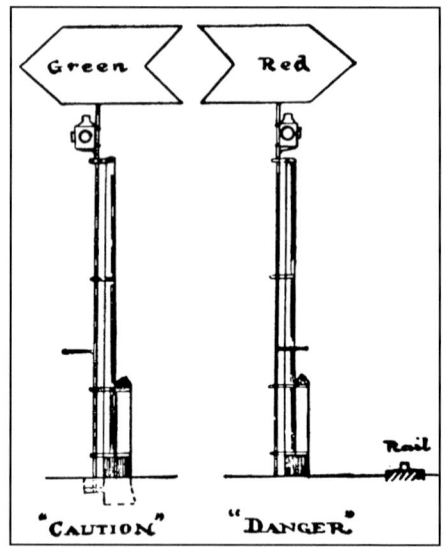

Left: Combined signal and point lever.

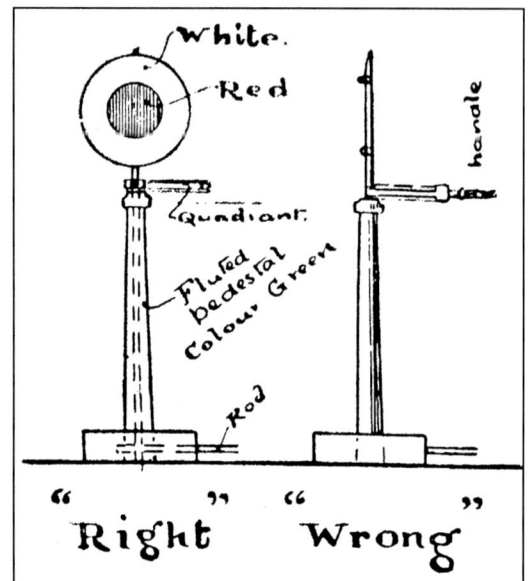

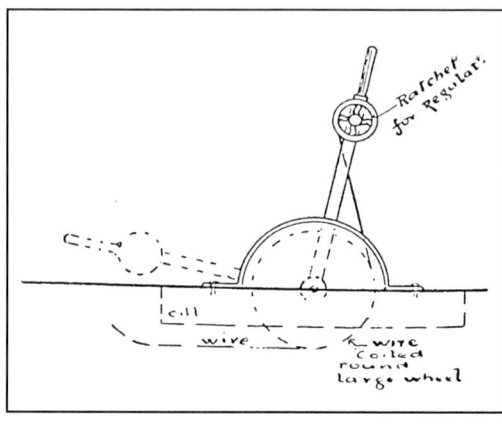

Ground lever for working outdoor signal.

Salisbury had but three signals; one at the passenger station's windscreen, another before the level crossing and the third 600 yards towards Wilton. That at the windscreen was abolished early and before the end of the broad gauge a semaphore Up signal came into use, controlled from the level crossing hut.

The single needle telegraph was placed in each station's booking office and generally one man trebled as signalman, ticket collector and telegraph clerk. The job was certainly not a sinecure: in addition to his duties in the station building, he was required to walk the length of the yard and padlock facing points and hinged blocks protecting sidings before pulling round the signals which, if interlocked with the points, required the exertion of considerable strength. At Wishford, Wiley, Codford and Heytesbury the office of station master was filled by a booking constable, whose uniform differed from that of a policeman, or switchman, in that an open collar replaced the regulation police collar.

Until 1874 porters wore a straw-coloured corduroy uniform, the shade being darker after that date. Fixed to their cap was 'GWR' in brass letters. Guards wore a long frock coat, its skirts embellished by sword flaps, red piping and brass buttons. Their distinctive cheese-cutter cap was ornamented by red bands. This semi-military style uniform harked back to the Royal Mail guard of the coaching era.

From 1874 crossing orders were used in conjunction with the disc block telegraph installed that year, but train staff and disc block

Staff at Codford 19th May, 1915. The large number was needed to deal with the war traffic.
Gerald Quartley

telegraph working superseded this on the single track sections in 1877 when signal boxes were built at Heytesbury, Wylye (with the modified spelling) and Codford, all having boxes that March. At this stage the investment did not include new loops.

In 1893 electric train staff operation was introduced on the branch. Speed restrictions of 3 mph were imposed at crossing stations for the single-line staff to be exchanged by hand.

As plans to remodel the LSWR's congested Salisbury station had implications for the GWR, an agreement was made on 28th January, 1898. The GWR laid a permanent double line junction to LSWR platforms No. 1 and No. 3 and built 'C' box with 93 working levers, this opening on 27th May, 1900. As there had been only partial interlocking in the GWR's Salisbury area, as a safety precaution trains in and out of the GWR terminus had to proceed at 4 mph for half a mile. This new box allowed the restriction to be lifted.

Name of Box	Year Opened	No. of Levers
Westbury Middle	1899	47
Westbury South	1899	74
		new frame 1914
Upton Scudamore	1900	17
Warminster	1904	37
Heytesbury	1877	34
Codford	1895	34
		new frame *circa* 1914
Sherrington	1914	14
Wylye	1877	?
Wishford	1895	23
Wilton	1895	27
Salisbury	1900	95

In 1899 Westbury was given three new signal boxes: Westbury North, originally equipped with an 82-lever frame, was modified in 1949 to 99 levers with VT5 bar locking. Westbury Middle had a 47-lever frame and Westbury South, located at the junction of the Salisbury and Weymouth lines, originally had a 57-lever frame, but was altered to 72 levers in 1914 and then 99 levers with VT5 bar locking in 1953.

The quadruple tracks between the North and South boxes were: the Up Weymouth; Up Salisbury; Down Weymouth; Down Salisbury, with the Up goods and Down goods loop laid respectively beside the Up Weymouth and Down Salisbury. The 1,644-foot long Down goods loop was opened in 1907 and the 2,478-foot Up goods loop in 1915.

The interior of Westbury North signal box
25th January, 1975. *W. H. Harbor*

Wishford station master, Wilf Talbot, in the station house garden *circa* 1955. *W. Talbot*

Wishford view Up in Southern Region days – note the upper quadrant signal. *Lens of Sutton*

On 27th-28th October, 1973, with the abolition of Salisbury C signal box, track facilities between Salisbury and Wilton were rationalised and track circuit block working introduced between Salisbury West and Wilton, and Wylye and Wilton, together with colour light signalling between Salisbury West and Wylye and absolute block working between Wilton and Wylye.

A panel was installed in the former parcels room in the 1860 Salisbury station building and brought into use during the week 17th-21st August, 1981. Initially it covered an area bounded by Grateley on the Basingstoke line, Dean on the Romsey line and Wilton on that to Warminster, but by the following year this had been extended to embrace Codford on the Warminster line. It replaced eight signal boxes, including the ex-GWR box at Wilton; Wylye closed on 28th August, 1981 and Codford 22nd June, 1982. Six signalmen worked the Salisbury Panel in shifts round the clock. In anticipation of this re-signalling, on 17th May, 1981 the Southern Region had taken control of 30½ miles of WR from Wilton to east of Sherborne, while in return the WR was given a length from north of Dilton Marsh to south of Warminster.

This new panel marked the end of signals and points hitherto operated pneumatically by low pressure air of approximately 15 lb per square inch. Initially the indication and detection of signals and points had also been carried out pneumatically, though latterly was electric. The new signalling was 3-aspect in the station area and 2-aspect beyond. Points were now operated by clamp lock machines except in the Wilton Junction area where Westinghouse M3s were used. In the event of a mains electricity failure, a back-up 50kVA diesel alternator came on automatically in the building which had once housed the air compressors. Passenger trains ceased to use Platform 1 and Down Platforms 3 & 4 were available for reversible working.

GWR crews normally worked through to the 17-siding East Yard on coal or freight trains for the LSWR, though if the yard was temporarily unable to accept them, a storage road was provided between the Westbury and Exeter lines west of the station to hold them while awaiting a path through the platforms. The East Yard, enlarged during the Second World War, handled all traffic from the WR and the West of England and marshalled it for destinations to the south and in the London direction. Technically all WR freight trains arriving were considered to terminate at Salisbury, but a few did continue southwards untouched except for the substitution of SR engines and crews. The SR's Salisbury West Yard handled all traffic to the West of England, while the former GWR Fisherton Yard handled all traffic for Westbury and beyond. Some half a dozen transfer trips were made daily between the three yards, and to economise, hauled where possible by an engine which had to pass through the station for operational reasons, so unlikely engines could act as Salisbury yard pilots.

LSWR crews with traffic for the GWR worked through to the Fisherton Yard west of the GWR terminus. Until 1900 the yard was controlled by two policemen, as the outdoor switchmen were termed, and were responsible for the signalling, locking of scotch blocks and point levers. A switchman also collected passengers' tickets at the ticket platform at the station throat. The man at the station end of the yard assisted with station duties. A white flag was exhibited at the level crossing for Up trains and green for Down. With the opening of the 'C' box, ticket collecting duties were carried out by the signalman, his box being adjacent to the ticket platform.

At Salisbury there were several point connections and one GWR signal where the working of the LSWR Salisbury West and GWR C boxes conflicted and thus required co-operation between the signalmen of the two companies. Due to the installation by the LSWR in 1902 of low pressure pneumatic signalling, chosen because the equipment could be maintained by mechanical fitters with no electrical knowledge, the interlocking between the two boxes required modification. In due course BR converted the pure pneumatic installation to electro-pneumatic by substituting electric circuits for control and indication, but retained compressed air for point and signal operation.

List of Signal Boxes

Distance Box to Box		NAME OF BOX	TIMES DURING WHICH BOXES ARE OPEN					Whether provided with Switch.
			Week Days			Sundays		
			Opened at		Closed at	Opened at	Closed at	
M.	C.		Mondays	Other Days				
—	37	} Westbury, North............	Open continuously.	—	—	—	—	No.
—	72							
—	13	Westbury, Middle	6.0 a.m.	—	—	—	11.0 p.m.	Yes.
—	22	Westbury, South	Open continuously.	—	—	—	—	Yes.
2	57	Upton Scudamore	Open continuously.	—	—	—	—	Yes.
1	51	Warminster ....{	Open continuously.	—	—	—	—	} Yes.
—	55	Beechgrove	6. 0 a.m.	6. 0 a.m.	10. 0 p.m.	—	—	Yes.
3	12	Heytesbury	6. 0 a.m.	6. 0 a.m.	10. 0 p.m.	—	—	Yes.
2	26	Codford ....{	Open continuously.	—	—	—	—	} No.
—	41	Sherrington Crossing	Open continuously.	—	—	—	—	} No.
3	35	Wylye ....{	Open continuously.	—	—	—	—	} No.
4	52	Wishford.................	7.30 a.m.	7.30 a.m.	7.15 p.m.	—	—	Yes.
2	37	Wilton...................	Open continuously.	—	—	—	—	Yes.
2	42	Salisbury ....{	Open continuously.	—	—	—	—	} No.

Opening times of signal boxes, from Service Time Table Appendices, 1945.

When the Southern Region took over the Salisbury line from the Western Region the ex-GWR box at Salisbury was renamed Salisbury C and its principal purpose was to regulate the block working of trains to Wilton North and Salisbury West in addition to shunting in the former GWR goods yard. Local coal traffic became more important following the closure of the SR's Milford Goods on 21st August, 1967, when its coal traffic was transferred there.

From opening until June 1861 Rowland Brotherhood held the maintenance contract supplying switches, crossing and other track parts. Holding maintenance contracts for other lengths of line, he cut the hay and kept sheep and cattle on the embankments making a '350-mile farm'. One year he raised and sold 40 oxen, 1,000 sheep and took first prize for the largest and best shorthorn cattle at the Chippenham and Warminster shows.

In the severe winter of 1940, freezing caused such severe problems to the signalling that the time-interval system had to be introduced temporarily.

Following the transfer of most of the line to the Southern Region in 1950, by 1963 about a quarter of the GWR lower quadrant signals had been replaced by the upper quadrant variety. As an economy all intermediate boxes between Westbury and Salisbury except Warminster, Codford and Wylye were closed in the 1960s, but Heytesbury and Wishford had been permanently switched out for several years.

56062 on crossover at Warminster to allow it to return to Westbury after banking 56050 on 13th June, 1988. The board reads: Assisted Trains Must Come to a Stand With the Train Locomotive at this Board. *Author*

Chapter Eight

Accidents

On 6th October, 1856 a train of 35 loaded cattle wagons containing sheep, oxen and heifers, arrived at Westbury at 6.00 pm. Due to its weight and the gradient ahead, it was decided to divide the train, two locomotives taking the first part to Warminster and then returning for the remainder. This plan was carried out, the two halves being reunited and then the train continued double-headed, leaving Warminster at 7.50 pm.

The engines were *Virgo*, a Leo class 2-4-0 and *Bergion*, a Premier class 0-6-0. The Westbury depot foreman knew that the driver of the second engine, Samuel Nicholls, did not know the road – it had opened less than four months previously – and warned him of the tricky gradients, but John Mays in charge of the leading engine said that he would take care of him because he had driven each of the fortnightly cattle trains.

Mays said that he stopped at Wylye for water and warned Nicholls that it could be dangerous going into Salisbury so the approach had to be taken steadily. Unfortunately Mays failed to keep his promise. The train ran away down the 1 in 99 gradient into Salisbury and although it should have gone into the goods yard, points turned it into the passenger station where it crashed into the buffers at the terminus and smashed through the brick and stone facade of the station's front. The *Salisbury & Winchester Journal* revealed that 'the floor and joists of the platform and walls of the ladies' waiting room were as clearly cut through as though it were the work of carpenters and masons.' The rear of the leading engine rested on the front of the second, which from the weight was embedded in the ground. Mays, thrown through the breach in the wall into the street was unhurt, but his fireman William Symonds jumped off, was concussed and needed to be carried to the Infirmary, while Samuel Nicholls and his fireman William Iles on the train engine were both fatally crushed between their locomotive and its tender. In addition 108 sheep were either killed outright or had to be slaughtered by the Salisbury butchers Judd & Dowding due to their severe injuries. Six dealers and drovers were also on the train, but they escaped only badly shaken. Station master Duffet used a Board of Health water hose to douse the locomotives' fires and thus prevented the timber station from going up in flames. As a safety precaution the gas lights were turned off, but this meant that all rescue operations had to be carried out by the light of candles or lanterns. The accident occurred about 8.30 pm and it was nearly 11.00 pm before all the danger was over.

During the night Mr Tarr, superintendent of the branch, arrived from Trowbridge and gave Driver Mays into police custody. At the inquest, Mays said that approaching Salisbury he shut off steam and applied the brakes at the usual place, but that the other driver still had his regulator open, either in forward or backward gear. The guards said that at Wilton, finding the speed too great, they applied the brakes. William Bond, a switchman at Salisbury, said that the train passed him at 30-40 mph, the first engine with its steam off and the second in reverse. Furthermore, no brakes were applied on either engine because, if they were, he would have heard them.

William Symonds, fireman on the leading engine, stated that he applied the brake, even though Mays did not tell him to do so. At the inquest Mr Appleby, superintendent of the GWR engineering department, said that the engine brakes were on, that the steam of the pilot engine was turned off and the train engine in reverse.

A verdict was brought in of accidental death, but the jury was of the opinion that the GWR directors were censurable in sending at night, engine drivers without an accurate knowledge of the road. Mays was released from custody. The jury recommended that the signal should be placed further from the station and Mr Tarr promised that a policeman would keep it at Red until it was seen that a train was under control.

One engine was removed by being partly dismantled. For some time the other remained embedded in the station.

A similar mishap occurred 14 years later, also at night, but on this occasion it was a passenger train which had insufficient brake power. Fortunately the collision was less severe and passengers escaped only receiving a shock, accentuated by the fact that some of the rape oil lamps were extinguished by the impact. The train was in charge of Driver Roffey, one of the first enginemen stationed at Salisbury who was easily identifiable as he wore spectacles, or 'barnacles' as they were popularly called, and were an unusual sight on a footplate at that period.

On 5th August, 1873, seven passengers were seriously hurt in a collision on the single line between Salisbury and Wilton, The trains involved were the 1.30 pm passenger from Bristol due to arrive Salisbury at 4.15 and the 4.35 from Salisbury, a mixed train for Chippenham which as far as Westbury, conveyed passenger coaches behind the goods wagons.

As the 1.30 pm from Bristol was telegraphed as being 36 minutes late at Warminster, Pinkerton, the Salisbury station master, not wishing to delay the 4.35 unnecessarily, wired to Wilton for a crossing-order to hold the 1.30 at Wilton, the message reading: 'The 4.35 Up mixed train ex-Salisbury will cross the 1.30 Down passenger train ex-Bristol at Wilton', the order being written on the standard form and countersigned by the Salisbury station master. As a check that the order had been received correctly, it was repeated by James Isaacs the Wilton station master. The ground switchman at Salisbury having been shown the order before it was handed to the driver, exhibited a white flag showing that Line Clear had been received from Wilton. At this period the reverse of the later practice was that the operator who *received* the signal pinned down the white or Line Clear key. The Salisbury switchman released the white disc and sent the 'Train on Line' signal followed by one beat on the bell. No answer was given and he was called away to alter points in the yard.

Meanwhile the 1.30 from Bristol had arrived at Wilton. James Isaacs, the Wilton station master was alone carrying out the task of ticket sales, managing the telegraph and signalling. Isaacs was discussing some official notices with Inspector Joseph Liddiard's son who was travelling on the 1.30 from Bristol, while some passengers were asking questions concerning LSWR connections. As Isaacs had had a harassing time the previous day dealing with 5,000 to 6,000 passengers when a big Bank Holiday fete was held in Wilton Park with Blondin, the tightrope walker being the star attraction, in a moment of forgetfulness the crossing order slipped his mind and he despatched the 1.30 off to Salisbury.

As it left, Isaacs suddenly realised his error that he had allowed two trains to enter a single line section, threw off his coat, made chase but was unable to stop it. Unfortunately he forgot the practice of 'flashing' the distant signal to attract a driver's attention. He rushed to the booking office and sent five beats of the bell – the Danger signal – but as mentioned above, the Salisbury switchman was out of his box and even if he had heard it, would have been unable to do anything to avert the accident.

The signalman in the nearby Salisbury LSWR box heard the bell and alerted his GWR counterpart to the circumstance, but by that time the brake whistles of the two trains were sounding, continuous brakes operated from the engine not yet in vogue. The head-on collision took place at Bemerton Bridge where the present A36 crosses the railway a mile west of the city. The speed of the mixed train had been reduced to nearly a walking pace and that of the Down passenger to about 15 mph.

The *Somerset & Wiltshire Journal* recorded that: 'The air filled with the piteous cries of the wounded and shrieks of terrified passengers'. The front brake van of the 1.30 was wrecked and pushed on top of the passenger engine's saddle tank resulting in the fatal injury of Guard William Tucker and also Driver Thomas Harvey, a regular driver of the 1.30 who was on *Homer*, a 4-4-0ST instead of his usual *Sun* 2-2-2ST. Driver Harvey was from the Bath shed and had had the honour of driving the first train through Box Tunnel. Driver Harvey and Guard Tucker died of their injuries on 24th and 26th August respectively. Driver Thomas Atkins of Chippenham shed and his fireman on *Gladiator*, a Standard Goods 0-6-0 heading the 4.35 from Salisbury, jumped off before the collision. Atkins escaped with a compound fracture of his left leg; his fireman was noted as 'seriously injured'.

Seven passengers also received severe injuries and a first class coach was sent from Salisbury to collect them. The most seriously injured were taken to Salisbury Infirmary and others sent to local hotels; a lady who had just married and was travelling to Australia with her husband had her teeth driven in. Passengers in the carriage attached to the goods train escaped with 'a good shaking' as the shock of the collision was deadened by the intervening wagons. Two passenger coaches were smashed to pieces as were two luggage vans.

When the GWR breakdown gang arrived on the scene they found LSWR men already at work clearing the wreckage. *Homer* was scrapped, but *Gladiator* was repaired and returned to service.

In his report to the Board of Trade Colonel Hutchinson said that the accident was due to the forgetfulness of the Wilton station master. Hutchinson believed that telegraphing should only be done by a regular signalman, and frowned upon the telegraph alone working a single line, adding that if both, or even one train had continuous brakes the consequences would have been less serious. The passenger train was headed by a Bath engine – its booked working began with the 7.30 am service to Bristol and then travelled to Chippenham and back before working the 1.30 pm to Salisbury and return, reaching Bristol at 9.00 pm when the locomotive and coaches returned to Bath, all with just one driver and fireman.

One of the outcomes of the inquiry was that all the points at Salisbury were made to work from the level crossing signal hut. Another recommendation was that trains should be more efficiently braked, but this was not implemented until a change of gauge saw fresh rolling stock.

Frederick W. Evans, secretary of the Bristol District Amalgamated Society of Railway Servants, wrote in *The Times* 17th August, 1874:

> Will you permit me to supplement the statements contained in my letter, published in *The Times* of 8th inst., referring to the management of the Wilton Station of the Great Western Railway since the fatal collision which occurred near there in August last, as it is probable that the attention of the President of the Board of Trade will be drawn to the subject at the reassembling of Parliament? When the inquiry into the cause of the two deaths was laid before the Coroner, a strong suspicion prevailed that had "starting" signals been in use at the station, they would probably have assisted the stationmaster's memory and so prevented the accident, as until such signals had been lowered the train could not have started, and the jury made a recommendation to the effect that such signals were really necessary for safety. Nor are the jury alone in their opinion, as the present stationmaster has applied to his superiors for

the erection of starting signals, but to no purpose. The recommendation of the jury and the stationmaster's appeal are equally unavailing when officers are anxious to keep down "the expenses". The assistance the stationmaster requires is to have two signalmen at the station to take charge of the "block telegraph" in use on the single line. At present he has to see to it all himself in addition to his other numerous duties, which together often keep him occupied without intermission for 15 hours. His hours of duty are from 6 a.m. till 10 p.m. In my previous letter I stated there was the 'same liability' to accident now as last year. I should have said 'more liability', the number of trains having increased since the conversion of the gauge from broad to narrow, which necessarily increases the stationmaster's duty. May I suggest that when human lives depend on one man's memory, 15 and 16 hours of daily toil is not the best incentive to carefulness on that man's part; and that a railway company which refuses to incur a slight outlay of money to secure the safety of its customers is not to be congratulated on its freedom from accidents through the faithfulness of its servants may hitherto have been the means of preventing them?

On the night of 20th August, 1874 a goods train from Bristol ran into a permanent way trolley between Wiley and Wishford, killing one man and seriously injuring three more. The *Salisbury & Winchester Journal* reported:

> It appeared that four men employed on the line, named George West, Richard Simper, and George and Oliver Smith, were proceeding along the line from Wishford Station in the direction of Langford on a trolly, [contemporary spelling] and that after going a short distance, the trolly was run into by a special train. The trolly was smashed in atoms, George West was killed on the spot, George Smith had his left hand so injured that it had to be amputated, Oliver Smith was injured about the back and Richard Simper escaped with a severe shaking. The wounded men were conveyed to the [Salisbury] Infirmary by the same train, and the body of West was taken to the Royal Oak Hotel, Wishford, where an inquest was held yesterday [21st August] before Mr R. A. Wilson, deputy coroner, and a jury, of whom the Rev. E. Hill was foreman.
>
> The first witness called was George Turner, ganger on the line, who stated that West, the deceased, was a foreman under him. On the previous evening he left the deceased at Wishford Station about half-past five, just after dropping work, and did not see him alive after. West had been in the habit of doing a little mowing after his railway work was done, for Mr Galpin, at Langford, whose place was situated about two miles long the line from Wishford. When he parted with him, Simper and George and Oliver Smith were with him. About ten minutes to nine he heard of the accident and went to the Station. He there saw George Smith, who told him that they had been run into, and he did not quite understand what he had meant. George Smith then explained that they had had the trolly on the line and that they had been run into. They had used the trolly before, and he had told them not to do it again. He saw West lying dead between the metals. Oliver Smith and Richard Simper were lying at the side injured. West lay nearly four feet from the others, and the trolly was smashed to pieces. The train had stopped at the station.

They got the trolly out of a hut near the station. The wheels and body of the trolly were locked by witness and the key placed where each had access to it. The deceased and his companions had no business with the trolly after work hours. The men on the line were always made aware when special trains might be reported to pass, and it was his duty every morning to ask what special trains might be reported to run in the courses of the day before going out with the trolly. The deceased and his companions had no right whatever to use the trolly after it had been locked without obtaining leave from him or from authority at the station; and he certainly did not give them leave to use the trolly after work hours.

John Hale, Bristol, driver of the engine deposed that he had been in the company's service for 12 or 13 years. He was in charge of a special cattle train from Bristol to Salisbury. He left Bristol at 5.35 pm on Thursday afternoon. All went well till he came into collision with the trolly. His speed at the time was about 25 miles an hour, which was about the normal rate. He saw an object on the line a few yards before the train came up to it, but he was not able to discover what it was. When the collision occurred he pulled up as soon as possible. The only sound he heard was that of the crash. There was a curve in the line where the collision occurred, and if the deceased and his companions had looked round they could not have seen the train approaching. The signals were all right at the station. It was 8.50 when the train pulled up. It came so suddenly upon them that he had not even had time to sound the whistle before the collision occurred. There were red lights on the engine.

Isaac Gage, fireman of the engine, who was the next examined, corroborated the evidence of the previous witness.

William Beckett, guard of the train, stated that his attention was first called to the occurrence by the break [contemporary spelling] whistle. He at once put on the break and on stopping he went back to see what was the matter. He met one of the injured men with his hand out walking towards the station. Further back he met another injured man being helped along, and shortly afterwards he found the deceased lying on his back quite dead. The jury at this point proceeded to view the scene of the accident. William Ditford, inspector of the permanent way, was then examined. He stated that Turner's duty was to manage the work on a certain length of line. The man had a rule book and a time table, and the rule on the matter was that the trolly was to be removed [from the track] a quarter of an hour before a train was due. The trolly ought to be off the line at half past five, and not be put on again till six the next morning, unless special orders were issued to the contrary. He was not aware that there had been a practice of using the trolly after hours, and if he had been asked by the men, he should certainly have refused.

Mr Wilson, in briefly summing up the evidence, pointed out that it was clear that the deceased and his companions were simply trespassers on the line, that they had already finished their work there, that the trolly had been locked for the night, and that they had unlocked it, and improperly and against the known rule used it to convey them along the line. He had reason to believe that the trolly was not unfrequently [sic] used after hours during the course of the harvest operations, and he thought it would be well if more stringent rules were made with a view to having the dangerous practice discontinued. It was quite clear that the men had no business on the line at the time, and it was also clear that the accident occurred through no fault but their own.

After a brief deliberation the jury found a verdict of "Accidental death" and recommended that in future all the men should not have access to the trolly key.

Superintendent Lydiard, from Bristol, and Inspector Morrison, from Trowbridge, attended on behalf of the company.

On 23nd September, 1898 a GWR coach was damaged at the LSWR's Salisbury station. The loaded GWR carriage coupled to a loaded LSWR carriage truck standing at the Down platform waiting to be attached to the 3.08 pm Down train, were struck by Adams T3 class 4-4-0 No. 568 running tender-first. Although there was no derailment, both vehicles were damaged and twelve passengers injured. The 4-wheeled third class carriage had carried a party from Teignmouth the previous day and was scheduled to return that party attached to the 11.45 am from Waterloo. The two vehicles could not be seen by signalman Edwin Ottaway in No. 2 cabin and forgetting their presence accepted the light engine, offered it to C cabin which accepted it and consequently he pulled off his home signal. Unfortunately with coal piled high in the tender, the sun in their faces, coupled with the fact that vehicles were on the middle road and the pillars supporting the verandah roof blocked the view, visibility from the No. 568 was poor and its fireman had not sufficient time to warn his driver to stop.

A head-on collision occurred at Warminster on 2nd September, 1916. A Down passenger train headed by Bulldog class 4-4-0 No. 3411 *Stanley Baldwin*, was shunted on to the Up line to enable the 8.45 pm mail service from Bristol to overtake, Fireman Harold John Edward Allen correctly placing a red light on the front of his engine. Meanwhile when the nine-coach 9.30 pm service Salisbury to Trowbridge, headed by 2301 class 0-6-0 No. 2557, due Warminster at 10.22 pm, arrived at Heytesbury, Signal-porter William Francis Bailey verbally warned Driver Ernest Stretch, 'Section clear; station blocked', this warning also heard by his fireman Percy Roy Staples.

Having departed and covered about three miles of track, Driver Stretch failed to see the Warminster distant signal at Danger, but observing the adverse home signal several hundred yards later, he called 'Whoa' and Fireman Staples applied the handbrake and Stretch the vacuum brake. The fireman had not spotted the distant signal as he was engaged in shutting off the injector. Speed was 20-25 mph, which would have been rather high for a train stopping at the station.

Seeing the approaching Salisbury train only about 100 yards away, after sounding the brake whistle the driver of the 8.50 pm Bath to Codford train jumped out – Driver Bert Davis was unhurt, but Fireman Allen damaged his back.

The engine of the 9.30 pm service struck headlong the engine of the Down passenger train shunted to the Up line. Neither locomotive derailed, but the first carriage of the Down train, full of soldiers returning to camp, telescoped over the tender of the engine ahead of it. This coach caught fire, probably ignited by a gas light although the gas was soon turned off. Troops collected water to douse the flames. Corporal Albert Hudson of the Royal Army Medical Corps was pinned down in the burning compartment of the carriage and although rescued he was dead when admitted to Sutton Veny Hospital at 11.10 pm. Ten other soldiers were taken to this hospital for treatment as was Driver Stretch of the Salisbury train who had suffered concussion when thrown off the footplate.

Next to the Salisbury engine was a milk van which was smashed to pieces taking the full force of the impact, the first carriage and its occupants only hurt by the jolt and broken window glass. Immediately the accident occurred, Sutton Veny Military Hospital was phoned for assistance. Officers and men soon arrived with ambulances and stretchers, but there were no broken bones, shock, cuts and burns being the chief injuries.

A breakdown gang from Swindon arrived at Warminster early the next morning and cleared the line that same day. Damage to rolling stock had been light – just to the front of the engines, while brake-third No. 382 was one of the smashed vehicles.

Publication of the Board of Trade accident report was delayed until after the trial and acquittal of Driver Stretch by Wiltshire Assizes. Lt. Col. Pringle said that the train travelled past the outer home at a higher speed than would be expected of a train which was booked to stop and had received a distant signal at danger. Fireman Staples said that the regulator was still open near the outer home. The warning whistle sounded by Driver Davis of the Bath train had roused Driver Stretch to the reality of his position and possibly caused him to shut off steam and apply the brakes, but no more than 100 yards separated the locomotives when this warning was given. For approximately 40 yards on the Salisbury side of the collision point a layer of sand was found along the rails indicating the driver had done his utmost to stop. The Divisional Locomotive Superintendent said records held nothing against Driver Stretch and that there were one or two commendations in his favour.

Driver Stretch had been on duty for less than two hours and had not worked an average of more than 60 hours weekly. He confessed to no domestic trouble and had rested in bed before coming on duty. He could not remember anything of what happened after the train stopped at Heytesbury, the collision throwing him off the engine and causing him to suffer from concussion.

Chapter Nine

First World War Military Branches

During the First World War two military branches were opened from the Westbury to Salisbury line. The contractor building a camp started by building a light railway from the nearest station to the site, the first being the 2¾ miles long branch from Codford station to Codford Camp. Constructed by Sir John Jackson Ltd, it opened in October 1914. At the Warminster end of Codford station it trailed northwards from the Down line before turning east. Locomotives used in the line's construction were: *Westminster*, a Peckett 0-6-0ST Works No. 1378 of 1914; *Codford*, a Hudswell, Clarke 0-4-0ST Works No. 720 of 1905; and *Prince Edward* a Manning, Wardle 0-6-0T Works No. 1064 of 1888

One of the locomotives working the line was a 1911 Avonside Engine Co Ltd 0-4-0ST *Finetta*, Works No. 1565, which came from the Teign Valley Granite Company *circa* March 1917. Post-war from October 1919 it was used at Sandford Quarry near Weston-super-Mare and at Conygar Quarry, Clevedon, the latter being on the Weston, Clevedon & Portishead Light Railway.

Dry store sidings, Codford Camp: open wagons with an extra three planks used for transporting horses. Circa 1914 the main line companies were each instructed to convert 400 open wagons for this purpose. The animals were required to face the direction of travel. Anzac troops are moving the stores. The engine is WD No. 16 *Finetta* Avonside Engine Co Limited No. 1565 of 1911 which worked the Codford Camp line between March 1917 and October 1919. She was eventually withdrawn from Imperial Chemical Industries Winsford circa 1953. Notice the shunter's pole across the buffers.

wylye-valley-postcards.co.uk

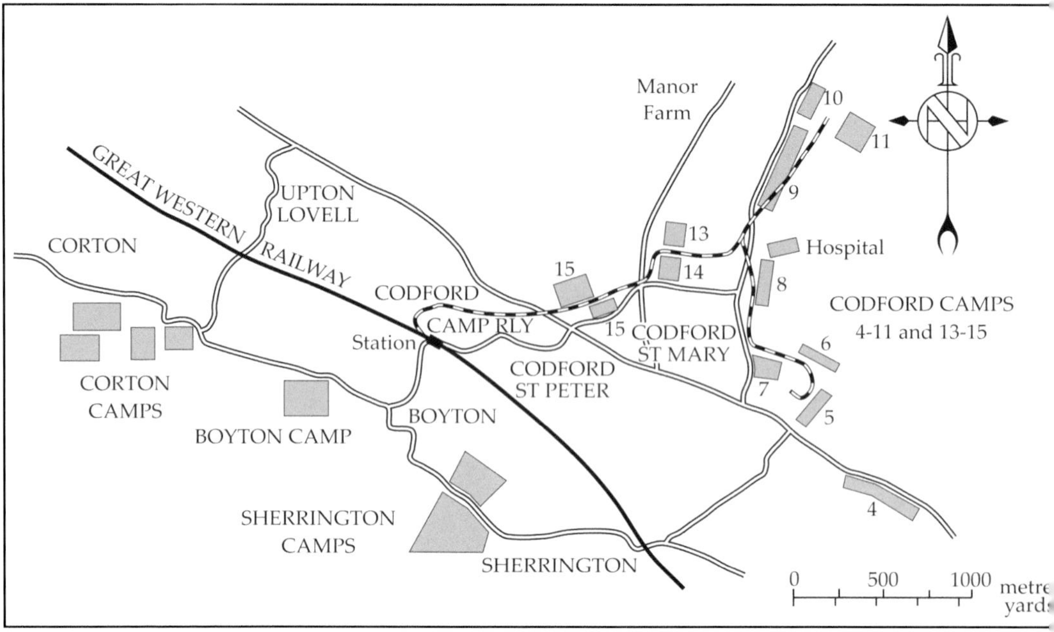

Plan of Codford Camp Railway

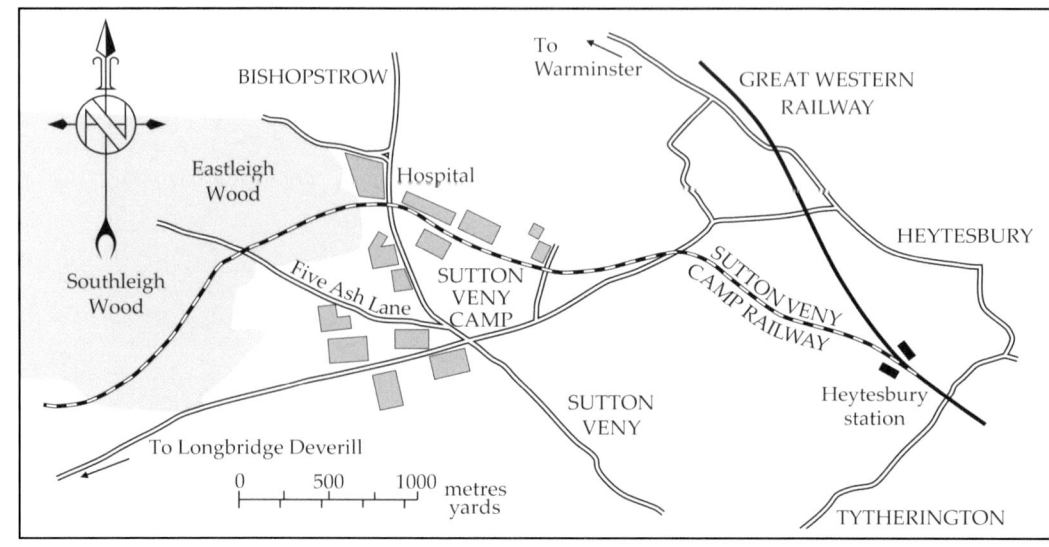

Plan of Sutton Veny Camp Railway.

FIRST WORLD WAR MILITARY BRANCHES

Workmen at Codford in 1915 for building the First World War military camps. View Down: notice the new shelter on the far right. Eventually there were 15 camps near Codford on the north side and seven on the south. It is to be hoped that someone is keeping a sharp lookout for an approaching train. *wylye-valley-postcards.co.uk*

On 29th October, 1915 stone ballast from Dulcote Quarry on the Cheddar Valley branch was to be delivered to the Codford Camp Railway and the GWR wrote to the War Department to inquire if the line was suitable for a GWR ballast engine, or whether a War Department engine should be used. It didn't receive a reply. The first train, consisting of 25 12-cubic yard ballast wagons ran on 3nd November, 1915.

The 4½ miles, including sidings, of the Codford Camp Railway, and the 5 miles of the Sutton Veny Railway were taken over by the War Office on 3nd June, 1916. Colonel Sinclair, commandant of the Longmoor Military Railway was responsible for the inspection, maintenance and operation of all the military camp lines. Except for the heaviest repairs, the military camp locomotives and rolling stock were maintained at Longmoor. The locomotives used on these lines particularly suffered from poor handling by often inexperienced crews over lightly-laid permanent way. Eventually management fell into the hands of the Director of Movements at the War Office, but Longmoor continued to provide repair facilities. The Codford Camps were numbered, not named, with the exception of Cyclists' Camp in the field through which the camp railway ran before reaching the present A36.

Codford Camp No. 13: track is laid on a field; the sharp curve has no check rail.

wylye-valley-postcards.co.uk

Codford Camp No. 6: a sentry is at foot of flagpole with a sentry box for shelter in inclement weather towards the right. A hand-pump is on the far right and the huts have telephone wires. The descent is steep and the permanent way light.

wylye-valley-potcards.co.uk

FIRST WORLD WAR MILITARY BRANCHES 143

The Codford Camp Railway crosses the Chitterne Road and climbs steeply to Camps Nos. 9, 10 and 11.
wylye-valley-postcards,co,uk

Circa 1915 the Codford Camp Railway crosses the Salisbury Road, now the A36.
Author's collection

In May 1918 the GWR took over working of the line from the War Department. A railway enthusiast raised in the 1930s was told that 517 class 0-4-2T No. 848 painted khaki was responsible. Following the Armistice, the Codford Camp line closed 1st January, 1923 and lifted by 1924 and very few signs of it can be seen today.

To facilitate further military requirements, about ¾ mile on the Warminster side of Codford was Upton Lovell where a workmen's halt was opened in November 1915, its siding from the Down line and ground frame having been opened 11th November, 1914. The siding was decommissioned about 1923 and lifted by 1925.

At Heytesbury station, the 3½ mile long Sutton Veny Camp line trailed from the Down line near the signal box, across the Up, continuing westwards for approximately 3 miles to Sutton Veny Camp. It was constructed by Oliver, Ling & Company in 1916-1917. No. 38 *Jersey Marine*, a 0-6-0ST Hunslet Works No. 869 of 1905 was used in construction and on the line's completion was sold to the War Department to work the branch together with *Glasgow*, a 0-4-0ST Andrew Barclay Works No. 185 of 1877. The line served a military hospital which opened in 1916. It consisted of lines of huts on a mile-long site, allowing ambulance trains to draw up alongside the operating theatres.

The line was taken over by the GWR in May 1918, two of the engines used being Caledonian Railway Lambie Class 1 4-4-0Ts No. 6 and 10 dating from 1893 and Westinghouse-fitted. GWR records state that they arrived on loan on 20th June, 1920 and both were on the allocation of Westbury shed on New Year's Day 1921, where they also carried out pilot work. No. 10 is recorded as moving to 'the Government' on 27th March, 1922, while No. 6 remained with the GWR at Westbury. Their return seems to have been in the spring/early summer of 1923 and classified as LMS 1P, saw out their time in Scotland before withdrawal in 1938 and 1932 respectively. The Sutton Veny Camp line closed and was lifted by 1926 except for a short length at the Heytesbury end which remained as a siding until lifted about September 1935.

Royal Army Medical Corps officers entraining wounded First World War soldiers. Ambulance trains were able to run from the Channel ports into Sutton Veny Camp to discharge patients within yards of the hospital wards. *Author's collection*

Construction in 1915 of the Sutton Veny Camp near Heytesbury; standard gauge wagons at the unloading area. The track is laid directly on a field. 2 feet gauge track on the left is used for distributing the building material. *Vowles*

The narrow gauge track has sharp curves and wide sleeper-spacing. Horses graze in the distance. How many men can you see on the motorbike? *Vowles*

Sutton Veny Camp Railway 1915: War Department 0-4-0ST *Glasgow*, Barclay works No. 185 of 1877 nearest. It had been used by Sir John Jackson Limited contractors for the nearby Codford Camp. WD No. 9 0-6-0ST beyond was obtained from the contractor who built the camp, Oliver Ling & Co Limited. It was inside cylinder Hunslet works No. 869 of 1905. Both engines are fitted with spark arresters. Ash wagons, left, have brought material for a better track base. The GWR Westbury–Salisbury is behind the line of distant trees. *Vowles*

Bibliography

Acts of Parliament
Backinsell, W. G. C., *The Salisbury Railway & Market House Company* (Salisbury: South Wilts Industrial Archaeology Society 1977)
Board of Trade Inspectors' Reports
Bradshaw's Railway Guides
Clark, R. H., *An Historical Survey of Selected Great Western Stations Volume Three* (Oxford: Oxford Publishing Company 1981)
Clinker, C. R., *Closed Stations and Goods Depots* (Weston-super-Mare: Avon-Anglia 1988)
Coleman, T., *The Railway Navvies* (London: Hutchinson 1966)
Cooke, R. A., *Track Layout Diagrams of the GWR and BR WR, Section 21 Bath and Westbury* (Harwell: Author 1987)
Cummings, J., *Railway Motor Buses and Bus Services in the British Isles 1902–1933* (Oxford: Oxford Publishing Company 1978)
Harrison, R., *Great Western Railway Locomotive Allocations For 1921* (Upper Bucklebury: Wild Swan Publications 1984)
Hateley, R., *Industrial Locomotives of Central Southern England* (Market Harborough: Industrial Railway Society 1981)
Leleux, S. A., *Brotherhoods, Engineers* (Dawlish: David & Charles 1965)
Leitch, R., *The Railways of Keynsham* (Long Stratton: RCTS 1997)
Lyons, E., *An Historical Survey of Great Western Engine Sheds 1947* (Oxford: Oxford Publishing Company 1974)
Lyons, E. & Mountford, E., *An Historical Survey of Great Western Engine Sheds 1837-1947* (Oxford: Oxford Publishing Company 1979)
McDermott, E. T. revised Clinker, C. R., *History of the Great Western Railway* (London: Ian Allan 1964)
Maggs, C. G., *The Bath to Weymouth Line* (Tisbury: Oakwood Press 1982)
Maggs, C. G. *Branch Lines of Wiltshire* (Stroud: Sutton Publishing 1992)
Maggs, C. G., *A History of the Southern Railway* (Stroud: Amberley 2017)
Mitchell, V. & Smith, K., *Salisbury to Westbury* (Midhurst: Middleton Press 1994)
Nicholas, J. & Reeve, G., *Main Line to the West Part One* (Clophill: Irwell Press 2004)
Oakley, M., *Wiltshire Railway Stations* (Wimborne: Dovecote Press 2004)
Phillips D., *The Story of the Westbury to Weymouth Line* (Sparkford: Oxford Publishing Company 1994)
Popplewell, L., *A Gazetteer of the Railway Contractors and Engineers of Central Southern England 1840-1914* (Ferndown: Melledgen Press 1982)
RCTS., *Locomotives of the Great Western Railway* (Various dates)
Richards, E. V., *LMS Diesel Locomotives and Railcars* (Long Stratton: RCTS 1996)
Robertson, K., *Great Western Railway Halts Volume One* (Pinner: Irwell Press 1990)
Robertson, K., *Great Western Railway Halts Volume Two* (Bishop's Waltham: KRB Publications 2002)
Ronald, Col. D. & Christiansen, M., *The Longmoor Military Railway* (Lydney: The Lightmoor Press 2012)
Rush, R. W., *British Steam Railcars* (Lingfield: Oakwood Press 1969)
Russell, J. H., *Great Western Diesel Railcars* (Upper Bucklebury: Wild Swan Publications 1985)
Thomas, D. St. J., *Regional History of the Railways of Great Britain, the West Country* (Newton Abbot: David & Charles 1981)
Vaughan, A., *A Pictorial Record of Great Western Architecture* (Oxford: Oxford Publishing Company 1977)
Wilts & Somerset Railway Minute Book
Wilts, Somerset & Weymouth Railway Minute Book

Great Western Railway Journals, particularly No. 26 article by Gerry Parkin; various *Railway Magazines*.

Appendix One

Westbury Shed Allocation

1st January, 1921

2-4-0 Barnum class	3207	3212	3219	3222		
4-4-0 Bulldog class	3340 *Camel*		3368 *Sir Ernest Palmer*		3407 *Madras*	
	3412 *John G. Griffiths*		3448 *Kingfisher*			
4-4-0 County class	3801 *County Carlow*		3815 *County of Hants*			
	3830 *County of Oxford*					
2-8-0 28XX class	2849					
2-8-0 ROD class	3037					
0-6-0 Standard Goods	1193					
0-6-0 Dean Goods class	2449	2450	2461	2468	2517	2541
0-6-0ST Buffalo class	735					
0-6-0PT 1661 class	1663					
0-6-0PT 1854 class	1856					
0-6-0PT 2721 class	2735					
CR locomotives	6	10				
Total 27						

(The *Locomotives of the Great Western Railway Part 14* says it is not known whether CR stands for Camp Railway or Caledonian Railway. Both these locomotives were at Westbury in March 1920. No. 6 was sent to Swindon Works in February 1923, while No. 10 had been sent 'to Government' in March 1922. The Caledonian Railway did lend some engines to the Government. If they were Caledonian Railway engines, they would have been Class 1 4-4-0Ts)

31st December, 1934

4-4-0 3252 class	3283 *Comet*					
4-4-0 3300 class	3316	3343 *Camelot*	3354	3384	3389	3421
4-6-0 Saint class	2933 *Bibury Court*		2977 *Robertson*			
4-6-0 Hall class	4932 *Hatherton Hall*		4964 *Rodwell Hall*		4982 *Acton Hall*	
2-6-0 4300 class	4314	4315	4326	4349	4365	4368	6341
	6382	6384	7302			
0-6-0 Dean Goods class	2394	2435	2518	2529	2566	
2-6-0 Aberdare class	2639					
0-6-0 2361 class	2364					
2-6-2T 4575 class	5511	5546	5556	5570		
0-6-2T 5600 class	5689	6690				
0-6-0PT 850 class	1915					
0-6-0PT 1076 class	1644					
0-6-0PT 1813 class	1816					
0-6-0PT 2721 class	2779	2780				
0-6-0PT 5400 class	5419					
0-6-0PT 5700 class	5718	6712	7711	7726	7727	7730	7749
	8722	8744				
0-4-2T 4800 class	4829					
Total 51						

31st December, 1947

4-6-0 County class	1027 *County of Stafford*		
4-6-0 Saint class	2928 *Saint Sebastian*	2941 *Easton Court*	2946 *Langford Court*
4-6-0 Star class	4028	4038 *Queen Berengaria*	4045 *Prince John*
4-6-0 Hall class	4926 *Fairleigh Hall*	4927 *Farnborough Hall*	4963 *Rignall Hall*
	5900 *Hinderton Hall*	5924 *Dinton Hall*	5925 *Eastcote Hall*
	5961 *Toynbee Hall*	5971 *Merevale Hall*	5974 *Wallsworth Hall*
	5985 *Mostyn Hall*	6966 *Witchingham Hall*	
4-6-0 Grange class	6804 *Brockington Grange*	6845 *Paviland Grange*	
4-4-0 Bulldog class	3363 *Alfred Baldwin*	3364 *Frank Bibby*	3438

2-8-0 28XX class	2803	2818					
2-8-0 2884 class	3842	3849	3850	3863			
2-8-0 ROD class	3014	3019	3032	3035			
2-6-0 43XX class	4365	4377	5306	5311	5326	6314	6351	6365
	6368	6369	6375	6399	7300	7302	7309	
0-6-0 Dean Goods class	2445						
2-6-2T 45XX class	4508	4520	4573				
2-6-2T 4575 class	5508	5509	5554				
0-6-2T 56XX class	5689	6690	6699				
0-6-0PT 2021 class	2053						
0-6-0PT 57XX class	5757	5771	5781	5785	7727	7784	
0-6-0PT 8750 class	3696	9612					
0-6-0PT 54XX class	5402	5419	5422	5423			

Total 71

1959

4-6-0 Hall class	4917 *Crosswood Hall*	4933 *Himley Hall*	4945 *Milligan Hall*
	5945 *Leckhampton Hall*	5963 *Wimpole Hall*	5974 *Wallsworth Hall*
	5975 *Winslow Hall*	6945 *Glasfryn Hall*	6955 *Lydcott Hall*
4-6-0 Modified Hall class	6994 *Baggrave Hall*	7909 *Heveningham Hall*	
	7917 *North Aston Hall*	7924 *Thornycroft Hall*	

2-8-0 2800 class	2811						
2-8-0 2884 class	3819						
2-6-0 4300 class	5358	6320	6358	7300	7302		
0-6-0 2251 class	2268						
0-6-2T 5600 class	5689	6625					
2-6-2T 4500 class	4536	4555	4567				
2-6-2T 4575 class	5508	5526	5542	5554			
0-6-0PT 5400 class	5414	5416	5423				
0-6-0PT 5700 class	3614	3629	3696	3735	4607	4636	4647
	5757	5771	7727	7748	7784	8744	
0-6-0PT 8750 class	3614	3629	3696	3735	4607	4636	4647
	9612	9615	9628	9668	9762		
0-6-0PT 6400 class	6408						
0-6-0PT 9400 class	8482						

Total 53

Appendix Two

Salisbury Shed Allocation

1st January, 1921

4-4-0 Bulldog class	3443 *Chaffinch*			
2-4-0 Barnum class	3217			
2-8-0 28XX class	2833	2844	2856	2877
0-6-0 Standard Goods	789			
0-6-0 Dean Goods class	2433	2565		
2-6-0 Aberdare class	2617	2671		
0-6-0PT 1076 class	1619			
0-6-0PT 1854 class	1704			

Total 13

31st December, 1947

4-6-0 Hall class	6955 *Lydcott Hall*	6978 *Haroldstone Hall*
0-6-0PT 8750 class	9628	

Total 3.

Appendix Three

Westbury Ironworks Locomotives

4 feet 8½ inch gauge

No.	Name	Wheel arrangement	Builder	Works No.	Date purchased	Date sold/ disposed
		0-4-0ST	Henry Hughes		c1874	?
		0-4-0ST	Henry Hughes		c1875	?
No. 7		0-4-0ST	Peckett	1099	1907	1937
	George	0-4-0ST	Andrew Barclay	1281	1912	1939
	Neptune	0-4-0ST	Andrew Barclay	1361	1913	1939

2 feet 0 inch gauge

No.	Name	Wheel arrangement	Builder	Works No.	Date purchased	Date sold/ disposed
No. 2		0-6-0ST	Hudswell, Clarke	167	1875	1924
No. 1	*Westbury*	0-6-0ST	Hudswell, Clarke	181	1876	1939
No. 3	*Cossington*	0-6-0ST	Peckett	753	1898	1939
		0-4-0ST	W. G. Bagnall	1725	1903	1917
No. 2		0-6-0ST	Avonside	1944	1924	1939

Appendix Four

Authorised Hours of Bank Engines 1954

Assists trains as required between Freshford and Upton Scudamore

Starting time 5.00am
19 hours on Mondays;
24 hours Tuesdays to Saturdays
6 hours Sundays.

Point to point time when running light
Warminster–Westbury 11 minutes
Upton Scudamore–Westbury 8 minutes

Appendix Five

Hand-Book of Railway Stations

Station	Traffic Classes in 1904	Crane power, changes to traffic clases and sidings		
		1904	1956	1962
Westbury	GPFLHC	2t 10c	12t 0c A. E Farr Siding War Dept Siding, Hawkeridge	
Dilton Marsh	–	–	P	
Warminster	GPFLHC	12t 0c	No change	Geest Industries Ltd Siding
Heytesbury	GPFLHC	1t 10c	Not listed	
Codford	GPFLHC	1t 10c	3t 0c by 1956 P: full truck loads of milk and empty milk cans	
Wylye	GPFLHC	1t 10c	P: passenger, parcels & miscellaneous traffic	P Crane removed
Langford	station not listed		Not listed	
Wishford	GPFLHC	1t 10c	Not listed	
Wilton North	GPFLHC	1t 10c	12t 0c P: passenger, parcels & miscellaneous traffic	P Crane removed
Salisbury	GPFLHC	12t 0c	GFL 12t 0c Crane	

Key to traffic accepted
G – goods station
P – passenger & parcel station
F – furniture vans, carriages, portable engines and machines on wheels
L – livestock
H – horse boxes, and prize cattle vans
C – carriages by passenger train

Appendix Six

Logs of Runs

Distance Miles	Time Min Sec	Station	Scheduled Arrival h m	Actual Arrival h m s	Scheduled Departure h m	Actual Departure h m s	Notes
\multicolumn{8}{l}{7 September 1957. No 6928 *Underlay Hall* 10 coaches Average speed: 36 mph}
–	– –	Salisbury	– –	– – –	6 53	7 7 20	
20	33 5	Warminster	7 22	7 40 25	7 24	7 42	Pulled up twice
4¾	8 13	Westbury	7 33	7 50 13	– –	– – –	

Total running time 41 minutes 18 seconds

Distance Miles	Time Min Sec	Station	Scheduled Arrival h m	Actual Arrival h m s	Scheduled Departure h m	Actual Departure h m s	Notes
\multicolumn{8}{l}{4 July 1961 No 7034 *Ince Castle* 9 coaches + 2 vans Average speed: 37 mph}
–	– –	Westbury	– –	– – –	9 29	9 35 50	
1¼	4 55	Dilton Marsh	– –	9 40 45	9 33	9 41 40	
3½	9 15	Warminster	9 42	9 50 55	9 44	9 54 50	
20	25 35	Salisbury	10 13	10 20 25	– –	– – –	

Distance Miles	Time Min Sec	Station	Scheduled Arrival h m	Actual Arrival h m s	Scheduled Departure h m	Actual Departure h m s	Notes
\multicolumn{8}{l}{4 July 1961 No 7925 *Westol Hall* 9 coaches Average speed: 41 mph}
–	– –	Salisbury	– –	– – –	5 35	5 40 45	
20	26 43	Warminster	6 2	6 7 28	6 4	6 9 30	Speed restriction Wilton
3½	5 49	Dilton Marsh	– –	6 15 19	6 12	6 16 17	
1¼	3 48	Westbury	6 15	6 19 55	– –	– – –	Signals

Distance Miles	Time Min Sec	Station	Scheduled Arrival h m	Actual Arrival h m s	Scheduled Departure h m	Actual Departure h m s	Notes
\multicolumn{8}{l}{21 June 1968 D7041 11 coaches (schools special) Average speed: 43 mph}
–	– –	Westbury	– –	– – –	– –	9 7 10	75 mph beyond Warminster.
24¾	34 10	Salisbury	– –	9 41 20	– –	9 41 20	PW slack Wylye

Distance Miles	Time Min Sec	Station	Scheduled Arrival h m	Actual Arrival h m s	Scheduled Departure h m	Actual Departure h m s	Notes
\multicolumn{8}{l}{21 June 1968 D7041 11 coaches (schools special) Average speed: 48 mph}
–	– –	Salisbury	– –	– – –	– –	6 53	
20	24 35	Warminster	– –	– – –	– –	7 17 35	Non-stop
4¾	6 40	Westbury	– –	7 24 15	– –	– – –	Non-stop

THE WESTBURY TO SALISBURY LINE

Distance Miles	Time Min Sec	Station	Scheduled Arrival h m	Actual Arrival h m s	Scheduled Departure h m	Actual Departure h m s	Notes
13 May 1975 W51303 etc 2 3-car DMUs Average speed 49 mph							
–	– –	Westbury	– –	– – –	10 9	10 9 20	
1¼	3 10	Dilton Marsh	– –	10 12 30	10 13	10 13 10	
3½	7 10	Warminster	– –	10 20 20	10 21	10 22 45	Stopped twice
20	20 20	Salisbury	10 43	10 43 5	– –	– – –	72 mph
13 May 1975 Nos 1102 & 1111 2 3-car DEMUs Average speed: 44 mph							
–	– –	Salisbury	– –	– – –	16 45	16 46 10	
20	24 35	Warminster	– –	17 10 45	17 11	17 12 40	20 mph speed restriction N. of Wilton
3½	5 5	Dilton Marsh	– –	17 17 45	17 16	17 18	
1¼	3 55	Westbury	17 20	17 21 55	– –	– – –	
26 May 2001 2-car DMU No 158871 Average speed: 58 mph							
–	– –	Westbury	– –	– – –	– –	9 20 32	Not scheduled to call at Westbury
4¾	6 13	Warminster	9 25	9 26 45	– –	9 27 41	
20	19 12	Salisbury	– –	9 47 5	– –	– – –	Not scheduled to call
11 June 2001 2-car DMU No 158821 Average speed: 56 mph							
–	– –	Salisbury	– –	– – –	19 12	19 19 4	
20	19 36	Warminster	– –	19 38 48	19 32	19 39 25	
3½	4 42	Dilton Marsh	– –	– – –	19 36	19 44 7	No call for request stop.
1¼	2 8	Westbury	19 41	19 46 15	– –	– – –	

Appendix Seven

TRAFFIC DEALT WITH

Station.	Year.	Staff. Supervisory and Wages (all Grades). No.	Staff. Paybill Expenses. £	Total Receipts. £	Passenger Train Traffic. Tickets issued. No.	Passenger Train Traffic. Season Tickets. No.	Receipts. Passengers (including Season Tickets, etc.) £	Receipts. Parcels. £	Receipts. Miscellaneous £	Receipts. Total. £
Westbury (Wilts.).	1903	45	2,691	15,374	41,047	*	4,275	770	1,674	6,719
	1913	64	4,966	22,530	51,669	*	6,004	822	2,923	9,749
	1923	130	22,251	40,062	64,134	537	10,918	1,229	4,228	16,375
	1924	132	22,063	39,189	62,015	668	10,960	1,306	6,304	18,570
	1925	123	22,278	41,218	66,882	723	11,088	1,450	8,799	21,337
	1926	123	21,515	36,373	60,579	569	10,259	1,732	7,368	19,359
	1927	129	24,270	37,128	67,119	524	10,777	2,102	4,724	17,603
	1928	†126	†23,026	35,490	69,836	599	11,131	2,503	4,198	17,832
	1929	†124	†22,603	35,821	70,184	646	11,010	2,767	4,719	18,496
	1930	†121	†22,624	34,809	68,850	587	11,199	2,400	4,845	18,534
	1931	†119	†21,783	33,533	61,927	605	10,082	1,758	4,224	16,064
	1932	†117	†20,831	28,481	55,894	640	9,473	1,538	2,066	13,077
	1933	†116	†20,340	25,406	52,791	647	9,006	1,576	803	11,385
Warminster..	1903	17	1,123	20,248	47,769	*	5,444	1,288	896	7,628
	1913	14	1,017	22,483	45,070	*	5,694	1,553	1,745	8,992
	1923	21	3,181	37,197	43,903	112	9,028	1,048	5,039	15,115
	1924	21	3,456	38,063	42,279	108	9,187	1,083	4,550	14,820
	1925	22	3,654	41,009	44,480	158	10,207	1,891	5,316	17,504
	1926	22	3,371	36,055	37,758	109	8,314	1,788	4,886	14,988
	1927	23	3,714	38,154	39,688	103	8,305	1,755	4,555	14,705
	1928	23	3,467	37,283	38,813	126	8,088	1,796	3,862	13,746
	1929	23	3,643	36,009	38,447	148	7,809	1,820	4,027	13,656
	1930	25	3,757	33,081	34,548	213	7,131	1,894	4,429	13,454
	1931	24	3,556	30,776	29,684	257	6,676	1,756	4,356	12,788
	1932	21	3,309	27,813	25,598	296	6,028	1,670	2,971	10,669
	1933	20	3,282	25,288	24,338	328	6,351	1,627	2,033	10,011
Heytesbury.. (†) Controlled by Codford from March, 1933.	1903	5	302	3,544	10,908	*	800	173	1,371	2,344
	1913	4	281	2,047	8,971	*	711	116	897	1,724
	1923	5	724	5,408	9,567	18	1,009	155	1,692	2,856
	1924	5	734	4,057	8,548	17	1,001	127	1,562	2,690
	1925	5	744	4,158	8,376	18	1,112	115	1,497	2,724
	1926	5	815	4,946	7,740	10	937	85	1,857	2,879
	1927	5	804	4,532	6,717	9	840	97	1,813	2,750
	1928	5	797	3,843	6,025	17	638	70	1,655	2,363
	1929	5	791	3,717	6,396	22	577	68	1,500	2,145
	1930	5	778	2,306	4,088	24	512	60	688	1,260
	1931	5	731	1,818	2,100	20	450	50	641	1,147
	1932	4	672	1,783	2,400	16	353	57	488	898
	1933	3	459	1,360	1,964	22	309	66	156	531
Codford ..	1903	10	443	3,185	10,539	*	883	208	211	1,297
	1913	9	526	3,555	10,594	*	942	123	338	1,403
	1923	10	1,351	9,449	8,758	27	1,221	200	2,100	3,521
	1924	10	1,371	7,024	8,076	26	1,206	166	2,658	4,030
	1925	9	1,340	6,088	7,830	46	1,098	150	2,038	3,286
	1926	9	1,274	6,847	6,166	36	954	144	2,307	3,405
	1927	9	1,323	5,478	6,192	42	867	185	2,315	3,367
	1928	9	1,276	5,031	6,025	46	845	206	2,254	3,305
	1929	9	1,301	5,810	5,750	30	732	237	2,294	3,263
	1930	9	1,254	4,709	4,743	34	500	225	2,073	2,888
	1931	9	1,204	4,306	3,278	33	438	166	1,841	2,445
	1932	9	1,161	3,373	2,462	39	407	175	1,128	1,710
	1933	9	1,142	4,595	3,748	36	887	214	1,182	2,283

* Not available.　　　† Including Telegraph Staff and Expenses from 1928.

GWR traffic dealt with at stations 1903-33.

AT STATIONS.

BRISTOL DIVISION.

\multicolumn{2}{c}{Forwarded.}		\multicolumn{3}{c}{Received.}	Coal and Coke "Not Charged" (Forwarded and Received).	Total Goods Tonnage.	Total Receipts (excluding "Not Charged" Coal and Coke).	Livestock (Forwarded and Received).	Total Carted Tonnage (included in Total Goods Tonnage).
Coal and Coke "Charged."	Other Minerals.	General Merchandise.	Coal and Coke "Charged."	Other Minerals.	General Merchandise.					
Tons.	Tons.	Tons.	Tons.	Tons.	Tons.	Tons.	Tons.	£	Wagons.	Tons.
46	1,351	2,598	10,573	4,212	7,155	10,491	36,426	8,655	180	2,711
134	12,355	3,004	6,173	5,058	7,003	7,178	41,505	12,781	159	4,098
375	9,987	2,080	11,989	18,627	8,073	14,236	65,367	23,687	61	2,784
284	10,064	2,130	9,713	4,600	9,502	3,641	44,934	20,619	55	2,978
345	13,245	1,759	8,284	3,517	8,902	7,145	43,197	19,876	62	2,881
831	3,456	2,119	6,420	4,795	9,343	5,481	32,445	17,014	80	3,202
699	3,248	1,984	8,036	5,057	11,102	6,580	36,706	19,525	129	3,736
223	3,197	2,311	7,390	3,750	9,538	6,920	33,338	17,058	50	4,121
227	4,777	2,567	7,401	3,152	8,198	8,165	34,577	17,325	57	3,911
314	3,815	2,376	6,794	1,692	8,225	8,458	31,674	16,275	59	4,240
363	4,132	2,231	6,241	7,013	8,607	9,083	38,270	17,409	31	3,883
471	2,635	2,159	7,211	5,647	8,561	7,778	34,462	14,504	19	3,701
481	2,806	2,700	7,764	964	7,504	7,635	29,854	14,021	19	4,651
—	1,005	7,037	8,332	3,742	15,152	3,590	38,858	12,620	318	4,637
39	347	7,695	7,457	7,299	15,327	5,124	43,288	13,491	436	4,682
135	830	6,939	4,107	7,605	13,555	9,079	42,250	22,082	607	3,311
18	246	8,169	4,874	8,713	14,977	9,652	46,649	23,243	525	3,510
28	291	8,475	5,880	9,451	14,582	9,164	47,871	24,105	423	3,818
77	1,001	6,301	3,786	8,208	14,397	7,518	41,288	21,067	427	3,216
58	1,196	7,267	5,026	7,430	12,644	10,597	44,216	23,449	427	3,154
41	443	9,202	5,087	4,245	14,285	8,737	42,040	23,537	435	2,999
112	612	8,351	5,273	4,433	11,231	9,525	39,537	22,353	420	2,984
181	350	6,776	3,924	5,341	10,818	8,135	35,525	19,627	409	2,600
52	174	6,603	4,618	3,263	9,873	8,169	32,752	17,988	358	2,506
—	189	6,036	5,084	2,631	8,251	7,379	30,270	17,144	331	5,383
—	278	4,768	3,943	2,616	7,843	7,000	25,950	15,277	327	6,405
—	44	904	1,003	438	1,245	468	4,102	1,200	107	278
9	—	395	892	844	819	761	3,720	1,223	173	217
10	71	1,184	156	634	681	1,006	3,742	2,552	64	266
—	17	325	178	1,082	920	1,201	3,723	1,307	65	172
7	48	557	189	1,249	654	1,079	3,783	1,434	62	172
9	167	504	135	3,220	791	583	5,429	2,067	79	178
—	335	874	125	1,597	765	944	4,140	1,782	57	165
8	164	300	52	938	483	682	2,627	1,480	123	83
—	561	246	106	1,524	459	671	3,567	1,572	52	78
—	858	128	72	56	271	543	1,928	1,046	56	55
—	60	67	119	338	298	531	1,413	701	42	54
—	115	51	86	110	536	522	1,426	885	64	140
20	10	108	74	14	348	628	1,402	820	22	198
—	237	1,322	487	796	1,832	679	5,353	1,888	73	580
—	—	2,063	391	1,388	1,877	1,067	6,786	2,152	116	601
—	8,339	1,599	149	710	1,277	999	13,082	5,928	145	320
—	5,320	1,013	311	1,071	1,180	1,019	9,914	3,894	108	223
9	—	1,788	169	1,228	1,225	930	5,349	2,802	118	247
10	64	1,848	103	2,614	1,247	603	6,480	3,442	136	238
—	100	767	93	1,574	1,228	907	4,669	2,111	119	196
—	119	1,005	102	2,052	1,040	909	5,227	2,626	195	109
—	120	840	139	1,128	1,186	857	4,270	2,547	178	110
—	38	531	113	410	1,126	914	3,132	1,821	164	110
—	—	247	129	371	1,401	922	3,070	1,861	160	106
—	57	334	174	154	1,474	951	3,144	1,063	105	503
—	—	551	154	61	2,219	1,025	4,010	2,312	117	1,447

TRAFFIC DEALT WITH

STATION.	YEAR.	STAFF.		TOTAL RECEIPTS.	PASSENGER TRAIN TRAFFIC.						
		Supervisory and Wages (all Grades).	Paybill Expenses.		Tickets issued.	Season Tickets.	Receipts.				
							Passengers (including Season Tickets, etc.)	Parcels.	Miscellaneous	Total.	
		No.	£	£	No.	No.	£	£	£	£	
Wylye	1903	5	323	3,526	11,483	*	971	177	661	1,809	
	1913	5	337	3,681	10,859	*	859	190	729	1,778	
	1923	7	1,081	6,001	9,529	41	1,176	326	1,205	2,077	
	1924	7	1,196	6,411	9,487	32	1,083	289	1,232	2,604	
	1925	7	1,188	6,416	9,238	35	1,116	303	1,399	2,818	
	1926	7	1,014	5,667	7,898	54	951	268	1,456	2,675	
	1927	7	1,153	5,855	8,276	54	987	265	1,454	2,706	
	1928	7	1,135	5,991	9,257	80	969	280	1,238	2,487	
	1929	7	1,119	5,884	9,062	68	914	279	1,246	2,439	
	1930	7	1,059	4,881	7,626	52	745	251	1,124	2,120	
	1931	7	1,042	4,821	6,848	32	661	240	935	1,836	
	1932	6	876	3,708	6,264	30	639	225	661	1,525	
	1933	6	895	2,828	5,314	29	585	214	171	970	
Wishford	1903	5	302	3,600	12,340	*	610	122	612	1,344	
	1913	4	270	3,149	10,943	*	515	74	271	860	
	1923	5	771	5,170	8,102	55	564	134	496	1,194	
	1924	5	780	4,774	7,654	62	530	132	439	1,091	
	1925	5	791	6,463	7,802	44	530	165	495	1,190	
	1926	5	737	5,474	6,654	30	438	136	467	1,041	
	1927	5	700	5,273	7,513	29	455	92	284	831	
	1928	5	777	5,471	6,863	23	394	134	302	830	
	1929	5	716	5,082	6,647	21	357	152	549	1,058	
	1930	5	755	3,883	5,942	19	312	155	566	1,033	
	1931	5	719	3,081	4,906	24	259	96	571	926	
	1932	5	704	3,027	4,740	31	254	110	376	740	
	1933	5	608	2,452	3,094	34	245	144	41	430	
Wilton	1903	5	323	3,269	22,994	*	702	165	196	1,063	
	1913	5	342	3,990	14,268	*	563	124	245	932	
	1923	6	983	7,077	4,956	19	670	148	255	1,073	
	1924	6	947	6,320	3,341	25	395	142	289	826	
	1925	6	975	7,176	3,529	28	445	135	212	792	
	1926	6	857	6,656	2,907	19	370	119	156	645	
	1927	6	994	8,740	2,298	21	324	118	182	624	
	1928	6	943	9,062	1,836	12	274	97	249	620	
	1929	6	937	8,666	1,863	2	240	118	208	575	
	1930	6	927	9,008	1,477	—	198	130	180	508	
	1931	6	890	8,014	1,240	2	168	178	193	536	
	1932	6	886	8,758	861	0	138	182	162	482	
	1933	6	907	6,808	865	3	150	146	158	463	
Salisbury (†)	1903	55	3,039	24,775	55,779	*	7,992	1,431	1,321	10,744	
	1913	41	3,296	28,221	50,710	*	8,041	1,138	1,236	10,415	
	1923	56	9,682	42,704	39,352	54	11,575	2,478	1,416	15,499	
	1924	55	9,962	45,043	36,613	39	11,379	2,570	958	14,907	
	1925	55	10,014	46,099	37,288	32	11,577	2,759	1,553	15,889	
	1926	54	9,019	43,554	34,639	17	10,946	2,287	1,436	14,669	
	1927	56	10,447	44,271	34,298	20	11,083	2,357	671	14,111	
	1928	57	10,241	49,320	32,297	32	10,821	2,318	1,721	14,860	
	1929	57	10,251	50,389	31,636	16	10,702	2,791	1,017	14,510	
	1930	59	10,501	48,606	28,052	19	10,066	2,772	889	13,727	
	1931	57	10,109	46,702	24,503	24	8,810	2,840	1,170	12,820	
	1932	49	9,194	45,252	21,584	23	7,751	2,587	984	11,322	
	1933	43	8,023	43,818	18,816	5	6,615	2,492	1,113	10,220	
Total	1903	102	5,855	62,147	171,812	*	17,402	3,559	5,268	26,229	
	1913	82	6,009	68,026	151,415	*	17,325	3,318	5,401	26,104	
	1923	110	17,773	113,006	124,167	326	25,243	4,489	12,203	41,935	
	1924	109	18,446	112,601	115,098	309	24,771	4,500	11,688	40,068	
	1925	109	18,715	118,009	118,543	361	26,175	5,518	12,510	44,203	
	1926	108	17,087	109,199	103,762	275	22,910	4,827	12,565	40,302	
	1927	111	19,225	112,303	104,082	278	22,951	4,869	11,274	39,094	
	1928	112	18,636	116,901	102,016	336	22,029	4,901	11,281	38,211	
	1929	112	18,758	115,557	99,801	307	21,340	5,465	10,841	37,646	
	1930	116	19,031	106,564	87,376	361	19,554	5,487	9,949	34,900	
	1931	113	18,251	90,548	73,064	401	17,465	5,326	9,707	32,498	
	1932	100	16,802	93,714	63,909	453	15,570	5,006	6,770	27,346	
	1933	92	15,406	87,149	50,030	457	15,151	4,903	4,854	24,908	

* Not available.

GWR traffic dealt with at stations 1903-33.

AT STATIONS.

BRISTOL DIVISION.

	Goods Train Traffic.									
Forwarded.			Received.			Coal and Coke "Not Charged" (Forwarded and Received).	Total Goods Tonnage.	Total Receipts (excluding "Not Charged" Coal and Coke).	Livestock (Forwarded and Received).	Total Carted Tonnage (included in Total Goods Tonnage).
Coal and Coke "Charged."	Other Minerals.	General Merchandise.	Coal and Coke "Charged."	Other Minerals.	General Merchandise.					
Tons.	Tons.	Tons.	Tons.	Tons.	Tons.	Tons.	Tons.	£	Wagons.	Tons.
—	177	1,755	742	420	2,284	1,054	6,432	1,717	168	274
—	12	1,555	867	308	2,829	934	6,505	1,903	164	292
—	10	1,556	288	476	3,267	1,622	7,214	3,294	76	217
9	—	1,558	223	1,289	3,187	1,706	7,972	3,807	158	213
9	18	1,884	172	1,204	2,806	1,758	7,851	3,598	149	248
—	15	1,162	178	1,035	2,632	874	5,896	2,992	159	208
7	97	932	186	1,931	2,786	1,800	7,739	3,140	94	186
—	17	1,258	263	2,011	2,564	1,589	7,702	3,504	176	91
—	118	1,192	251	1,986	2,121	1,623	7,361	3,445	154	77
—	111	745	226	480	2,347	1,365	5,274	2,761	115	106
—	211	419	122	1,594	2,383	1,541	6,270	2,985	112	83
—	268	404	115	974	1,696	1,465	5,012	2,183	83	806
—	247	314	179	334	1,801	1,331	4,206	1,858	54	1,263
—	175	1,694	939	1,138	3,339	1,914	9,199	2,256	28	365
—	—	1,802	850	1,103	2,899	1,806	8,460	2,289	86	344
—	—	2,384	217	791	2,560	2,472	8,424	3,076	95	287
7	—	1,539	232	1,905	2,732	2,681	9,096	3,683	101	304
—	80	2,714	276	4,380	2,664	2,605	12,728	5,273	105	373
—	—	1,720	270	3,209	2,544	1,564	9,307	4,433	127	301
—	154	1,154	184	2,066	2,522	2,580	9,560	4,442	125	316
18	100	1,475	232	4,843	2,110	2,537	11,315	4,641	115	185
—	340	1,148	320	4,570	1,641	2,660	10,679	4,024	75	183
—	285	962	274	468	1,530	2,693	6,212	2,850	78	164
—	167	527	229	244	1,352	2,844	5,363	2,155	81	117
7	144	454	243	1,510	933	2,971	6,262	2,287	74	353
—	209	599	158	1,141	938	2,870	5,915	2,022	70	674
7	—	1,551	1,988	1,116	1,028	3,068	8,753	2,206	175	604
9	9	4,625	1,021	321	1,273	3,500	10,848	3,053	193	629
30	1,342	3,985	1,878	545	1,360	3,164	12,304	6,004	202	472
17	1,243	3,418	1,449	843	1,458	3,799	12,232	5,503	142	632
7	331	5,693	1,373	1,754	1,448	3,861	14,467	6,384	214	693
32	242	4,510	674	2,376	1,438	2,798	12,070	6,011	230	623
54	674	4,086	859	4,538	2,276	4,351	16,838	8,116	219	662
18	485	4,661	899	5,002	2,645	3,833	17,633	8,442	248	554
20	789	4,189	1,043	5,552	2,050	3,368	17,011	8,001	292	599
17	263	4,246	1,165	8,876	2,240	3,307	20,114	8,500	211	612
7	203	3,382	1,222	6,928	2,103	3,096	16,891	7,473	266	620
—	109	3,330	1,103	12,454	2,032	3,775	22,803	8,276	211	877
12	545	2,890	1,185	7,662	1,961	3,866	18,121	6,345	165	898
30	182	6,705	6,790	3,296	10,354	18,335	45,701	14,031	879	5,210
168	1,660	5,809	8,085	3,796	12,529	25,989	58,036	17,806	1,122	6,696
235	374	4,973	7,897	3,223	11,790	23,716	52,208	27,235	600	6,474
205	460	6,006	9,170	4,579	14,417	29,663	64,500	30,136	452	7,814
140	474	7,371	7,545	3,673	13,414	30,749	63,366	30,210	853	8,033
204	246	6,576	5,845	4,024	13,176	26,270	56,341	28,885	800	7,690
170	655	4,683	9,749	4,927	13,140	29,071	62,404	30,160	840	6,486
236	1,705	4,784	9,446	6,982	13,461	25,360	62,004	34,460	1,077	6,525
346	1,775	4,364	11,095	9,241	16,408	25,619	68,848	35,879	763	6,757
272	1,167	3,894	9,780	6,297	17,739	25,142	64,201	34,969	852	6,583
337	1,203	2,653	12,335	4,779	18,029	27,452	66,788	33,882	744	6,602
318	1,354	2,358	15,473	7,024	17,408	26,483	70,418	33,930	825	7,400
280	1,279	2,086	16,680	10,462	15,532	26,696	79,045	33,598	504	9,172
46	1,820	21,058	20,276	10,946	35,234	29,108	118,488	35,018	1,748	11,948
225	2,028	23,944	19,568	15,059	37,553	39,271	137,643	41,922	2,290	13,401
410	10,966	22,620	14,687	13,993	34,490	42,058	130,224	71,071	1,879	11,347
256	7,286	22,028	16,437	19,487	38,871	49,721	154,086	71,633	1,551	12,868
200	1,242	28,482	15,604	22,948	36,798	50,146	155,415	73,806	1,024	13,584
332	1,755	22,621	10,901	24,686	36,625	40,210	136,820	68,807	2,057	12,454
296	3,211	19,263	16,222	24,963	35,361	50,250	149,566	73,209	1,881	11,165
351	3,033	22,685	16,081	26,163	36,588	43,647	148,548	78,690	2,369	10,546
478	4,385	20,330	18,227	28,434	35,096	44,323	151,273	77,911	1,943	10,797
470	3,072	17,282	15,554	21,928	36,071	42,099	136,476	71,574	1,885	10,239
396	2,018	13,848	18,774	17,517	35,430	44,555	132,547	67,050	1,763	10,088
325	2,236	13,057	22,873	24,863	32,430	43,546	139,325	66,368	1,692	15,462
312	2,563	11,315	22,373	28,200	30,374	43,416	138,649	62,241	1,319	20,057

INDEX

Aberdare 24, 94, 120
Act of Parliament 5 *et seq.*, 11 *et seq.*, 31, 33
Allen, Harold John Edward 137
ambulance train 38, 39
Amesbury 86
Andover 6 *et seq.*, 18
Anglo-American Oil Co 71
Appleby, Superintendent 132
Arriva Trains 94
Atkins, Thomas 133 *et seq.*
atmospheric railway 7, 9
Avonmouth 122
Awdry, Sir John Wither 9

Bailey, William, Francis 137
Barnes & Tanner 12
Basingstoke 7 *et seq.*, 14, 72, 128
Basingstoke & Salisbury Railway 33
Bath 8 *et seq.*, 47, 58, 107
Beckett, William 136
Beechgrove, Ordnance Depot 55
Bertram, J. H. 50
Bicester 122
Bishopstoke (Eastleigh) 7 *et seq.*
Biss Bottom 24
Blackwall, Thomas Evans 31
Blondin 133
Board of Trade 7, 17, 76, 134, 138
Bond, William 132
Botley 122
Bournemouth 86, 115
Bradford-on-Avon 5, 7, 9, 11. 56, 95, 115
Brassey, Thomas 5, 33
Bratton 40
Brereton, R. P. 11, 18, 58
Bridport 9
Brighton 92, 115
Bristol 7 *et seq.*, 20, 22, 24, 43, 47, 50, 58
Bristol & Exeter Railway 7 *et seq.*, 86, 105, 115
Bristol & North Somerset Railway 19
Bristol & South Wales Railway 32
Bristol, South Wales & Southampton Union Railway 31 *et seq.*

British Railways 34, 44, 47
Brotherhood, Peter 31
Brotherhood, Rowland 12, 14, 31, 41, 130
Brunel, I. K. 5, 7 *et seq.*, 72
Buford 86
Bullo Pit 120
Bus 12, 40

Cardiff 39, 61 *et seq.*, 68, 75, 86, 88 *et seq.*, 92, 112 *et seq.*, 122, 139 *et seq.* 153, 156 *et seq.*
Chichester 122
Chippenham 5 *et seq.*, 18, 32, 120, 130
Codford 18, 22 *et seq.*, 24, 30, 36, 111. 117, 125 *et seq.*, 128, 130
Codford Camp Railway 29, 63 *et seq.* 139 *et seq.*
Crawley 122
Creed, John 57
Cuncliffe, A. P, 67
Cyclebag 92

Davis, Bert 137 *et seq.*
Davis, Frank 57
Davies, G. Morley 57
Devizes 5, 7, 9, 105
Dilton Marsh 40, 44 *et seq.*, 128, 153
Ditford, William 136
Dorchester 7
Duffet, stationmaster 131
Dulcote Quarry 141
Dunn's seeds 34
Durston 7

Eastleigh 5, 18, 122 *et seq.*
English China Clays 71
English, Welsh & Scottish Railways 81
Evans, Frederick, W. 134 *et seq.*
Exeter 122

Fane, Revd. Arthur 15
Fareham 122
Firbank, J. T. 81
Freightliner 81
Frome 5, 7 *et seq.*, 12, 35, 40 *et seq.*, 50, 86, 99

Gage, Isaac 136
Galpin. Mr 135
Gauge conversion 20, 107, 109
Geddes, J. 35
Geest 91
Gillingham 80
Grant, G. 120
Great Western Junction Railway 7
Great Western Railway 5 *et seq.*, 12, 14 *et seq.*, 19, 30, 32 *et seq.*, 40, 86, 108 *et seq.*, 119, 121, 126, 129, 144
Green, Candida, Lycett 47
Grovely Wood 66
Gyngell, Messrs 14

Hale, John 136
Hamilton, William Peter 30
Harvey, Thomas 133
Havenhill, Mr 31
Herbert, S. 31
Heytesbury 9, 18, 22 *et seq.*, 24, 30, 37, 50, 55, 58 *et seq.*, 95, 97, 111, 122, 125 *et seq.*, 130, 144, 153, 156 *et seq.*
Hill, Revd. E. 135
Hoof & Hill 5
Hudson, Corporal Albert 138
Hunt, Christopher 92
Hutchinson, Colonel 134

Iles, William 131
Isaacs, James 133 *et seq.*
Isle of Wight 8

Jackson, Sir John 139
James, William 7
Jones, H. P. 24
Judd & Dowding 131

Kelsey, Alderman 17
Kineton 122

Lake, Barry 68
Langford 17, 66, 135, 153
Lavington 6, 18
Liddiard Mr 133
Little Langford 15

LOCOMOTIVES
GWR Classes: 481 85; 517 85, 144; 717 85; 14XX 89; 2301 137; 28XX 42. 89, 95 *et seq.*; 3000 96; 38XX 101; 4073 1, 45, 63, 67, 89 *et seq.*, 104; 42XX 90, 96; 43XX 49, 96, 98; 45XX 122; 47XX 87; 49XX 60, 63, 87, 89 *et seq.*, 99, 117; 53XX 49; 54XX 89; 56XX 1, 45, 49, 53, 87, 89, 96, 98; 57XX 89, 95, 122; 72XX 89 *et seq.* 96 *et seq.*; 8750 101; Aberdare 95; Atbara 86, 95; Badminton 86, 88; Barnum 65, 67; Bogie 83; Buffalo 95; Bulldog 95, 137; County (4-4-0) 89 *et seq.*; County tank 100; Dean Goods 89, 102; Duke 85; Fire Fly 83; Flower 86; Grange 87, 90 *et seq.*; Hawthorn 83 *et seq.*; Leo 14, 83, 87, 131; Manor 87, 89; Metro 22, 36, 84; Premier 83, 131; Saint 87; Standard Goods 26, 63, 83, 133; Star 86 *et seq.* ; Sun 83, 133 *et seq.*; Steam railmotor 86, 112, 114; Diesel railcar 87, 116
BR Classes **Steam:** Britannia 87, 89; Class 4 89; Class 5 90; Class 9 89, 91
Diesel: Hymek 39, 90 *et seq.*; Warship 59; Western 79, 92; Type 3 91; Hampshire DEMU 91, 118; InterCity 121; Swindon Cross Country 91; Class 31 91; Class 33 91 *et seq.*, 118; Class 47 101; Class 59 98; Class 66 98; Class 70 98; Class 101 56; Class 127 92; Class 155 92, 94, 118; Class 156 92, 118; Class 158 92 *et seq.*; Class 159 104
LMS Classes: 2F 0-6-0 96; Class 5 101; Jubilee 91; Class 8F 70, 87, 98
LNER: *Mallard* 91
LSWR/SR: A1/X 34; B4 34; D15 86; G6 34; M7 34; N 87, 91; O2 34; Q1 91; S15 90;
T3 137; T9 70, 86; U 86, 90; 0298 34; 0395 34; 348 103; 415 34; 700 34; Battle of Britain 56, 90; West Country 89 *et seq.*, 104

London & Southampton Railway 5 *et seq.*, 16
London & South Western Railway 5, 7, 16, 33, 68, 72, 75 *et seq.*, 80 *et seq.*, 112, 114, 121, 126, 129
Long, Walter 8
Longmoor Military Railway 141
Ludgershall 122
Lydiard, Superintendent 137

Mahon, W. 33
Marchwood 122
Mays, John 131 *et seq.*
Mead, R. J. 44
Meldon Quarry 122
Melksham 7
Meredith, Captain 10
Merehead 122 *et seq.*
Midland & South Western Junction Railway 67
Milford 76, 80. 130
Ministry of Defence 55
Mitchell, J. 15
Morrison, Inspector 137

Nationalisation 30
navvies 10, 15, 17, 41
New Passage 3, 32
Newbury 7
Newport 120
Newton Tony 86
Nicholls, Samuel 131
Nine Elms 5

O'Brien, Captain William 11
oil burning locomotives 113
Oliver, Ling & Co 144
Opening 6, 11 *et seq.*, 17 *et seq.*, 31 *et seq.*, 50
Ottaway, Edwin 137

Paddington 35, 68
Page, Alphonse Le 56 *et seq.*

Patchway 32
Patney & Chirton 35
Pinkerton, station master 132
Plymouth 35
Pole, Sir Felix 30
Pope, W. G. 62
Portskewett 31 *et seq.*
Portsmouth 8, 18, 23, 30, 39, 68, 75, 112, 120
Pringle, Lieutenant Colonel 138
Prosser, James 57

Quidhampton 10, 71, 122

Radstock 7 *et seq.*, 17, 20, 41
Railway Mania 5, 7, 11
Rank, J. V. 67
Reading 14, 35
Regional Railways 81
Richardson, Charles 32
Roach & Pilditch 10
Roberts, Mrs H. 47
Roffey, driver 132
Royal Electrical & Mechanical Engineers 55

Salisbury Electric Light & Supply Co 34
Salisbury 5 *et seq.*, 17 *et seq.*, 19, 22 *et seq.*, 33, 36, 47. 50, 71 *et seq.*, 86, 88, 94 *et seq.*, 102 *et seq.*, 115 *et seq.*, 120 *et seq.*, 130 *et seq.*, 137, 152 *et seq.*, 158 *et seq.*
Salisbury & Yeovil Extension Act 7
Salisbury Market House Railway 33 *et seq.*
Saunders, Charles Alexander 8, 11, 16 *et seq.*
Scott, J. 23
Severn Bridge 120
Severn Tunnel 23, 32, 120
Sherborne 9
Sherrington 22, 64, 126
Simonds, H. 13
Simper, Richard 135
Sinclair, Colonel 141
Smith, George 135
Smith, Oliver 135
Snow 23 *et seq.*

Southampton 7 *et seq.*, 18, 19, 23, 30, 75, 86, 111, 120, 122
Southampton, Bristol & South Wales Railway 19
Southern Electricity Board 34
Southern Region 30, 44, 53, 55, 68, 81, 130
South Wales Railway 31
Stallard, Revd. G. 15
South West Trains 81, 94
Staples, Percy Roy, 137 *et seq.*
Staverton 9
Stockton crossing 64, 66
Strapp, John 35
Stretch, Ernest 137 *et seq.*
Strike 10, 23 *et seq.*
Sutton Veny Camp Railway 30, 61, 138 *et seq.*
Swindon 6 *et seq.* 18, 22, 24, 68, 120
Sylvester, F. T. 57
Symonds, William 131 *et seq.*

Tarr, Superintendent 132
Taunton 35, 122
Taylor, Messrs 11
Tennear, J. R. 43
Thingley Junction 5, 7, 9, 11
Thring, James 17
Tinkerpitt 71
Titt, J. Wallace 53
Tommy shop 10
Trowbridge 9, 40, 58, 86, 115, 117, 119, 120, 122

Tucker, Henry 57
Tucker, William 133
Turner, George 135

Upton Lovell 22, 61, 144
Upton Scudamore 1, 11, 19, 22, 37, 44, 45, 48, 49 *et seq.*, 56, 90, 94, 120 122, 126

Wales & West 48, 81, 119
War Department 30, 55, 87, 141, 144
Ward, R. J. 9, 11, 17
War Office 31
Warminster 5, 7 *et seq.*, 11 *et seq.*, 22 *et seq.*, 30, 37, 40, 47, 50 *et seq.*, 86 *et seq.*, 91, 94 *et seq.*, 104 *et seq.*, 119, 122 *et seq.*, 126, 128, 130 *et seq.*, 137 *et seq.*, 148, 153, 156 *et seq.*
Waterloo 18, 68, 94, 119
Wentloog 122
West, George 135
Western Region 30, 44, 55, 129 *et seq.*
Wessex 81, 94, 119
Westbury 7, 10 *et seq.*, 18, 20, 22 *et seq.*, 26, 29 *et seq.*, 35 *et seq.*, 47, 50, 58, 68, 89 *et seq.*, 94 *et seq.*, 99 *et seq.*, 111, 119 *et seq.*, 126 *et seq.*, 131, 148, 150 *et seq.*

Westbury Iron Works 20, 37. 40 *et seq.*
Weymouth 5, 7 *et seq.*, 22, 45, 48, 119
West Wilts Rail Users' Group 94
Whatley 122
Willcox, Dr. 59
Willesden 122
Wilson, R. A. 135 *et seq.*
Wilton 18, 22 *et seq.*, 36, 67 *et seq.*, 105, 107, 111 *et seq.*, 126, 128, 132 *et seq.*, 153, 158 *et seq.*
Wilts & Somerset Railway 57
Wilts Friendly Society 105
Wilts, Somerset & Weymouth Railway 5. 7. 9 *et seq.*, 22, 35, 4, 124
Wishford 18, 22, 30, 36, 66 *et seq.*, 111, 125, 127, 130, 135 *et seq.*, 153, 158 *et seq.*
Woking 122
World War, First 30, 55. 61, 139 *et seq.*; Second 30, 34, 38, 53, 99, 128
Wylye 1, 18, 22 *et seq.*, 26, 30, 64 *et seq.*, 68, 107, 125 *et seq.*, 130 *et seq.*, 135 *et seq.*, 153, 158 *et seq.*

Yeovil 7 *et seq.*, 24
Young, Mr. 23
Yolland, Colonel 17

43XX class 2-6-0 No 5385 heads the Saturdays-only 2.45 pm Westbury -Warminster 2nd July, 1955. The train is composed of 2 auto-coaches. The sleeper-built Down platform of Dilton Marsh Halt is on the left.   *R. E. Toop*